Encouragement and Inspiration for the Times of Our Lives

A FIRESIDE BOOK
Published by Simon & Schuster

New York   London   Toronto   Sydney   Singapore

Love Someone Today

DELILAH

with Dave Newton

FIRESIDE
Rockefeller Center
1230 Avenue of the Americas
New York, NY 10020

Copyright © 2001 by
Jones Broadcast Programming, Inc., and Delilah

Second Fireside Edition 2002

FIRESIDE and colophon are registered trademarks
of Simon & Schuster, Inc.

For information about special discounts for bulk purchases,
please contact Simon & Schuster Special Sales:
1-800-456-6798 or business@simonandschuster.com

Designed by Ruth Lee

Manufactured in the United States of America

1   3   5   7   9   10   8   6   4   2

Library of Congress Cataloging-in-Publication Data
Delilah, date.
Love someone today : encouragement and inspiration for the times
of our lives / Delilah, with Dave Newton.
    p.   cm.
1. Interpersonal relations—Religious aspects—Christianity.
2. Delilah, date.   I. Newton, Dave, date.   II. Title.
BV4597.52.D45 2001
248.4—dc21
00-065413

ISBN 13: 978-0-7432-1716-3

Acknowledgments

There are so many people I want to thank for helping to take this book from dream to reality: Tami Mutal and Jean Lange, who collected, sorted, and organized our listeners' letters; Dave Newton, who had to deal with my occasional tirades as we worked through each poem, each letter, each story together; our editor, Nicole Diamond, who sought us out and proposed that I write a book, and had the dedication and tenacity to see it through.

I also want to thank Ken Spitzer and Mike McVay, who took me from unemployment (after I was fired from my twelfth station) into national radio; and Edie Hilliard, Jim LaMarca, and the people at Jones Broadcast Programming, who bought the show from Ken and Mike and grew our network from twelve stations to over two hundred.

I owe so much to my producer, friend, and confidant, Janey. Without her and our assistant producer, Peter Ward, there would be no radio show, since, in reality, they do most of the work and I get all the glory.

Finally I want to thank God. Because of His grace, His mercy, and His undying love, I am here today. I have been blessed beyond measure.

To my precious children,

Sonny, Manny, Tangi, TJ,
Shaylah, and Zachariah—

with all my love

Contents

To everything there is a season,
And a time to every purpose under heaven:
A time to be born, and a time to die;
A time to plant, and a time to pull up what is
   planted;
A time to kill, and a time to heal;
A time to break down, and a time to build up;
A time to weep, and a time to laugh;
A time to mourn, and a time to dance;
A time to cast away stones, and a time to
   gather stones together;
A time to embrace, and a time to refrain from
   embracing;
A time to get, and a time to lose;
A time to keep, and a time to cast away;
A time to rend, and a time to sew;
A time to keep silence, and a time to speak;
A time to love, and a time to hate;
A time of war, and a time of peace.

ECCLESIASTES 3:1–8

Introduction

I come from a long line of gift givers. My grandpa Mac is in his eighties. He has a pacemaker and he weighs less than one of my young teenagers, but you can't leave his house empty handed. When someone stops by to visit, whether it's family or a casual friend he met at his cancer support group, they leave laden with gifts. He'll go to the pantry and pull down a bag of dried beans he raised before his health failed him, or fill a sack with sweet corn in the summer—he still keeps a small garden plot next to the house. When I was growing up he and Grandma kept a huge garden, an orchard, and a few head of cattle.

At least six species of berries grew on their little farm. When you drove away after a visit your backseat and your trunk were filled to the brim with crunchy apples, sweet peas, huge heads of cabbage, snap beans, tender sweet carrots, and a few steaks from the deep freeze. If Grandpa had gone fishing early that day, you'd leave with a fresh salmon or a trout packed in a Styrofoam cooler on the seat next to you.

My father's family was much the same. They gardened, fished, and dug clams almost every day. When Grandpa Luke wasn't out on the water he was working in his wood shop; he was a master craftsman. He turned out glorious handmade myrtle-wood bowls, platters, and candleholders.

While he worked amidst the curled wood shavings, my grandmother was in the house crocheting. Granted, her color schemes left something to be desired, but us grandkids always had a new hat to wear on the always chilly Oregon beach, a new comforter to throw on our beds. My family wasn't rich, but they always had something to give to others.

As I got older I discovered I didn't enjoy the carful of corn nearly as much as the time spent with Grandma Mac in the garden while she picked it. I rarely wore Grandma Luke's orange-and-lime-green stocking caps, but I loved to watch her fingers fly as she made them. I discovered it wasn't the gift nearly as much as the time that went into it that really mattered.

Over the years, I have received some wonderful gifts: extravagant bouquets of yellow roses, cut crystal bowls, lead-glass clocks. I've won awards and plaques and gift certificates to exquisite restaurants. But the most precious gifts I've been given are less tangible—the gifts of time I've been granted by God, time spent with those I love.

And they haven't all been pleasant times. The lessons I have learned from times of struggle, times of confusion, and times of pain have all been gifts that have helped me to become who I am.

The times I've spent alone have helped me to appreciate the true gifts of marriage, family, friendship, and motherhood. Time spent with my children, my grandparents, my mother, my brothers and sisters, my husband, and my friends is far sweeter as a result. Even time spent with a complete stranger, connecting in some small way, is a beautiful gift worth treasuring.

When I was in my twenties I was driven by ambition. I felt a need to prove myself to my strict, demanding father and to others whose approval was vital to me. I wanted to succeed, and I worked hard at my job. But in the difficult and capricious world I chose, it matters little how hard you work or how good you are at what you do. The average stay of an "air personality" at any one radio station can be as brief as eighteen months. In other words, you get fired a lot, and I was no exception. In fact, I've contributed generously to that statistic.

It took years, and more than a few mistakes, before I really, truly realized the value of time and how important it is to spend it wisely, to invest it. I began to understand that the things we most treasure are not necessarily *things* at all. I heard a man named Mike McKorkle speak one day, and the gist of his talk was this: In the end, there will be only two questions God will ask you. What did you do with me? And what did you do with the people I put in your life? He'll want to know if you loved them. Did you care for them? Did you spend time with them? These questions still burn in my heart.

So, my house is usually something of a disaster. I would much rather invest time watching my infant son learn to pull himself up into the kitchen drawers than organize them. I would rather watch my daughter create wonderful works of art for our refrigerator than hang the collection that's been stored in my attic forever.

I love spending time with my husband, talking about everything and nothing. Sometimes, when the kids are in school and we can find a baby-sitter for the two younger ones, we go out on a date for lunch or walk along the beach near our home. I value these gifts of time far more than the little gold earrings he gave me for Christmas.

I love spending time with my sister and her family. I'd

rather spend an afternoon in her cozy backyard having a picnic than going to a movie or a Broadway play . . . well, maybe I could go to the picnic and then to the play!

The sad thing about these gifts of time is, we often don't recognize them for what they are until the moment is past. We don't savor the moment, the hour, the week until years later, when it might be too late to acknowledge the gift.

I have a friend who is also in radio. She got a phone call one night from a lonely young woman who had been kicked out of her parents' home some years past. The woman said something profound: "If I had known it was my last night at home, I would have enjoyed it more." How often do you feel that way?

If I had known it was my last time talking with my brother on the phone, just before his plane crashed, would I have enjoyed the conversation more? Would I have said something that needed saying? If I had known how fast my children would grow, would I have enjoyed the hours watching them sleep more? Would I have spent more time walking with them through the woods looking for imaginary wild animals, and less time ordering them to clean their rooms?

Time is, at its core, a gift of love. Every night on the radio, I encourage my listeners: "Love someone." One of the easiest ways to show someone how much you love them is to give them your time. The time we spend with others, the small moments we share in our busy lives, are the most precious gifts we can give or receive.

But even more important, you must know that time is always passing. When you fully understand this, you'll never let a moment of it get away from you without making sure you're caught in the act of giving love to someone. It can't wait until tomorrow.

This book is my gift of time and love to you. I hope it will help you to become more alert and watchful, to recognize the gifts you are given as they arrive, moment by moment, and to use them, savor them now, today. The more watchful you are, the more alive you'll be, and the more vivid and sweet will be the memories you'll have, to keep.

When you see an opportunity to share your time with others—your parents, your children, or the stranger you run into on the street—I hope you'll embrace it passionately, giving your time freely and enjoying it to the fullest. My hope is that this book will inspire you to worry less, perhaps work less, organize less, and spend more time connecting with the people in your life, giving of yourself and showing them your love.

If you knew this were your last day, what would you do?

A Time to Be Born

$\mathcal{I}$ have to wonder. Did Eve give any thought to us, her daughters of decades to come, when she decided that foolish apple was something she just had to have? With a garden full of pineapples and pomegranates and papayas and passion fruit, why did she go for that which was forbidden? The Bible reports that after she heard that delectable crunch, tasted the sweet fruit, felt the juice running down her chin, there were, shall we say, a few unpleasantnesses. One of my least favorites of these is this: "To the woman He said, 'I will greatly multiply your pain in childbirth, in pain you will bring forth children.'"

I have heard people say that if childbirth's pain were not

erased from our memories, there would never be brothers or sisters, just "only children." If we women could remember the sensations of labor and delivery, we'd sleep alone and wear chastity belts for the rest of our natural lives. Victoria's Secret would go out of business. I wouldn't have a job playing sappy, romantic, sexy love songs on the radio.

I believe Bill Cosby understood the process well when he suggested men imagine what a woman goes through in child-birth this way: "Take your lower lip . . . and pull it up over your head."

Some things get easier—even better—as we age. Like sewing or cooking, crocheting or gardening. But certainly not childbirth. At twenty-four I modeled . . . right into my fifth month of pregnancy. I worked in the yard and in the garden until a week before my son was born. I took long walks and swam every other day.

At thirty-four I got a little more tired, but still I managed to sand and refinish our hardwood floors in my eighth month, and I took my son camping in the woods, too.

I noticed a few varicose veins on my legs when I was carry-ing my daughter, but still felt sexy enough to pose for preg-nancy pictures in a gauzy white maternity shirt. And little else.

I delivered Shaylah at eleven-fifteen at night. I was released from the hospital less than ten hours later to go home and snuggle. I was up and dressed for church the following day. Like I said, that was at thirty-four.

At thirty-nine I wanted to sleep. And eat. And sleep some more. And eat some more. That's all I wanted to do. I was as big in my fifth month as I had been when I delivered the other two . . . looking at me, you would have thought I was carrying a twenty-pound baby. The once-few varicose veins on my legs now looked like an L.A. freeway map. Complications developed and I had to stay in bed the last five weeks. Which wasn't so bad, since all I wanted to do was eat and sleep.

Nursing a baby at my fortieth birthday party was something I had absolutely never dreamed of doing. My goddaughter—my best friend's little girl—came to my party. With her boyfriend. Wearing a promise ring. She's off to college and I'm nursing a baby.

But even with the hemorrhoids, L.A. freeway veins, sagging breasts, stretch marks, fat stomach, and flabby bum I've developed as a result of childbirth, I have only one regret: I didn't experience the honor of the horror of birth with the three kids we've adopted.

Still, when I get to heaven I am definitely having a talk with Eve about that fruit thing.

DELILAH

When I was four years old my family lived in a rented farm-house in the Oregon countryside. Our landlords, the Mikul-eckys, had a collection of old cars and trucks and farm equipment standing around, rusting in the wet Northwest weather.

There was an antique Model A Ford sitting halfway be-tween their house and ours. It was off-limits to us kids. Their son planned to restore it one day and didn't want us climbing in and out of it, doing further damage to the already dilapi-dated automobile.

It was late at night, or at least it seemed late to a four-year-old, and I was fresh out of a hot bath. My mom came to tuck me into bed, and I reached for Kissy Baby, my one and only doll.

She wasn't there on my bed. She was not in the little cradle my father had made. She was not in the bathroom, nor was she on the couch. She was nowhere to be found. I couldn't sleep without Kissy in bed with me. I sobbed hysterically as my folks frantically searched for my precious doll.

Suddenly I remembered where I had last seen Kissy—in the backseat of the old Ford. The old rusting Model A. The off-limits car. Now I had a dilemma. Did I confess that I had broken the rules and gone into that car, and risk a spanking? Or did I try to make it through the night without my baby doll? There was no question, really. The thought of my blue-eyed baby out in the cold night air, alone where bugs and mice might be attacking her sagging stuffing, was enough to make me confess.

Muttering, my mother found a flashlight and set off into the night to find Kissy. In a matter of minutes the doll was back in my arms, and tearfully I fell asleep.

Kissy wasn't much to look at. Her head, arms, and legs were made of plastic. Her cloth body was little more than a pillow. Most of her once-blond locks had been pulled out because I used them as a handle. When she was new she had a music box buried in her stuffing, with a little wind-up key on the back. When she was wound, her head and arms moved with the lullaby. But after a few months of hugging and holding and dragging through the mud, she needed a few repairs. Mom performed surgery after I had fallen asleep, making an entire new body for her and removing the broken music box.

For years I had but one prayer: "Please, God, make Kissy a real baby, not just a doll." I would kiss her good night, close my eyes, pray hard, and when I woke up the next morning I'd check for signs of life. And I hadn't even heard of Pinocchio. Every night I prayed, and every morning I'd wake to find her eyes as glassy blue as the night before.

When I was four my mother got pregnant, and when DeAnna was born, with bright blue eyes, I thought for a while that God might have answered my prayers. But after a few weeks she started to fuss and whine, and after a few months she was only happy if she was being held by Momma, and I knew she wasn't the real baby I had asked to be mine.

And then I got older, and my best friend at school became more important than Kissy Baby. After a while Kissy stopped sleeping in bed next to me, ended up on the floor and finally in the closet. I got older and a million other things became more important, and finally I forgot Kissy altogether. But my desire to be a mom was something I never lost.

When I was twenty-one I met the man who would become my son's father, and we were married a year later. My heart's desire was to have a child. He was not nearly so enthusiastic; he already had two children and wasn't as involved in their lives as he had hoped to be. Our marriage was strained from day one. He couldn't see where having another child would make things better. I was young and naïve. I thought if we had a child he would want to parent the baby as much as I did. Or maybe I was so set on getting what I wanted that I didn't really take his feelings into consideration much at all. I simply wanted to have a baby to love and to raise.

Shortly after our son was born, I was a single parent. But I had no regrets then, nor do I now. Sonny was the best thing that ever happened in my life. It was because of him that I found my faith in God above, and it was because of him my life turned around. From the very moment of conception I was in love, completely and totally, with the baby growing in my belly.

I told my friend Robin, "This child is going to be special. He is going to be a leader of men." She thought I was crazy. Funny . . . faith and religion were the furthest things from my mind back then, but I knew in my soul and in my spirit that God had a special plan for Sonny's life. When he was born I looked into his deep, black eyes and I saw his future.

To this day I have never met anyone with a heart as pure or a nature as sweet as my firstborn's. I don't know what he will become, but I do believe that my prophecy many years ago will come true. He is going to help to change the world by his goodness.

After Sonny was born I longed to have more children, but for years I was a single parent, just the two of us together. When I met Doug we talked a lot about our plans and hopes; we both knew we wanted a big family. We knew we wanted to adopt children together, but we also hoped to have a biological child.

We were married less than a year when God blessed us and I became pregnant. I was ecstatic, but all the while I had a horrible fear, a secret fear I could barely admit to myself, let alone anyone else. I was afraid I wouldn't love another child as deeply or as completely as I did my first. He was my heart, my soul. How could I possibly love another child as intensely as I did Sonny? But when I gave birth to Shaylah and held her to my breast, I began once again to fall in love. It took a few more weeks with her than with Sonny, but I was relieved to realize there is plenty of room in a mother's heart for more than one child.

Her golden blond hair felt like heaven against my cheek, her bright blue eyes met mine with wonderment and love. She is a brilliant little girl. She was talking and singing by the time she was only a year old. When she says, "I love you, Momma-bear," I feel as if I have already arrived in Paradise.

When Shay was only a month old, my mother came to visit. When she arrived she brought some things with her that she had packed up from our attic at home. I opened one musty-smelling box to find an old scrapbook, my pom-poms, my diary, and Kissy Baby. She was wearing the little paisley dress Mom had made for her when we lived on the farm, and her eyes were still just as blue. Holding her worn cotton body in my hands, I remembered the prayers I had uttered thirty years before: "Please, God, make her real." I looked up from the ancient doll in my hands to my blond, blue-eyed baby lying in her bassinet, and I realized my prayers had finally been answered.

None of us is born without risk. And life is never trouble free, any more than it's joy free. I can offer plenty of proof. My friends—my listeners—share their lives with me and one another every night. I couldn't leave them out of this book, any more than I could keep them off the air. They surround me, like a family.

One of them, Sharon, knows a lot about what society thinks of as the perfectly natural, even routine act of becoming a mother, but she knows more than most of us do about the risks. When her Kaytee Michelle was born, two years ago, everything seemed to happen like clockwork. Sharon and her husband were ecstatic.

*W*hen she was born I had so many plans for her, so many things I wanted to do for this beautiful baby girl who depends on me for absolutely everything.

Then, when she was three months old she got bacterial meningitis and suffered two strokes on the left side of her brain. This left her blind, and she was diagnosed with cerebral palsy. She also lost her ability to suck and has to be fed through a tube in her stomach. She can no longer hold her own head up.

I went through so many emotions, and I still do. I think the hardest things we have to deal with, other than her not being able to see, are the simple little things, normal things we do every day and take for granted. These are all the things that my beautiful baby has lost.

One night during her crisis, we were sleeping in the waiting room of the hospital pediatric ICU and we were awakened and told that Kaytee would not make it through the night. The rest of our family was called. My baby brother arrived. His wife had given birth to a baby boy a week before me. He hugged me with all his might and said, "Is there anything I can do?"

I told him, "Hold your baby so very close and don't let him go regardless of what happens . . . he can be taken from you so soon." I want to share that same advice with you. Cherish every second.

There was a day just recently that I was so overwhelmed with stress and grief I couldn't stand it. I was sitting here thinking how much easier it would be if I just walked away, ended this game that was dealt to me . . . and then I looked over at Kaytee and she gave me the biggest smile! She hadn't smiled in a year until that moment. That smile said to me, *Thanks, Mommy, you're doing a great job!* I know now that I'll have bad days and good days, but just looking back on that smile holds me together.

We spent a long time in the hospital with Kaytee—she spent four weeks on life support and stayed there to recover for three more months. We spent that time thinking about how our hopes for our little girl getting the most out of life were shattered. But through the grace of God and powerful prayers, we've come to realize that though Kaytee faces many challenges, not everything has been taken from us, nor have we been crushed. We were so selfish about what we had lost that we were too blind to what we got to keep. Each time I hold my baby, or sing to her, or give her a bath . . . or tell her how much I love her . . . I remember how lucky I am. We got to experience joy twice in a lifetime—Kaytee being born, and Kaytee living on.

On a Thursday I went to the clinic for my ultrasound. Shaylah went with me, of course . . . she went to almost all my appointments with the midwife. She was full of questions, fascinated with the baby growing in my belly. Shaylah had all but decided this was going to be her baby.

The technician turned the computer screen so Shaylah and I could both have a great view of the little miracle. In a matter of seconds we could see the baby's head and face, all of its tiny, delicate features. I couldn't help but cry as the baby kicked and moved, more than a growing lump in my belly . . . an actual little person I would be holding in my arms in just a few months.

When Sonny was in my womb I didn't get to watch the full ultrasound. I was given only a small photo that I really couldn't make out. When I was pregnant with Shaylah the midwifery program did ultrasounds only in emergencies. So this was my first real experience seeing a baby before I gave birth.

At one point the baby's hand shot forward past its little face, and it seemed to be waving. Shaylah waved and squealed, "Hi, baby! I'm your big sister!"

I started to cry and tried to wipe the tears from my face. Shaylah said, "Momma-bear, your face is wet with happy!"

It was my third pregnancy, my third birthing experience. I thought I was completely prepared. I had packed my bags weeks before, realizing that since labor had arrived early with my other two children, the likelihood was pretty good it would take me by surprise this time around as well.

My firstborn ended up being a C-section, but my second childbirth was a beautiful, all-natural experience that made me appreciate life in a new and miraculous way.

I talked with Doug and my midwives to develop our birthing plan. We wanted to have our two girls in the room with us—Shaylah was four, and our foster daughter, Tangi, was twelve.

I packed scented candles and some of my favorite CDs to listen to while I labored. We bought frozen fruit bars that I would eat during the process, and we had nonalcoholic champagne chilling in the back of our fridge, ready for the big celebration.

But in the words of Robert Burns, "The best laid plans o' mice and men . . ." Sometimes God steps in and takes over, and your plans go flying out the door. So it was with my birthing plan. It went flying out the door, and so did I.

I had prayed for a quick and easy labor, forgetting just how faithful God can sometimes be about answering our prayers. Wednesday, April 14, I went to the midwives' for my checkup. My blood pressure had been running high for a few weeks, so they were closely monitoring me. When I arrived it was high once again, and they decided that since I was already full-term, they would induce me.

They sent me over to the hospital, where the midwife gave me a dose of gel to get me going. After watching me for about two hours, they sent me home and told me to return at eight the next morning for a second dose.

Doug took me home, and we even stopped along the way for Thai food. We got home about nine and I was so tired I went straight to bed. At about eleven I woke up feeling some contractions, but nothing too serious. About an hour later my friend Janey started to time them; they were coming about five minutes apart. So I got up, trimmed my bangs—I haven't a clue what inspired that—woke Doug from his nap, and called my friend DJ, and asked her to bring the girls to the hospital to join us.

Doug didn't think there was any rush, since I was feeling fine when I woke him at twelve-thirty. But within a few minutes, my chipper disposition disappeared. Our departure could be described as an only slightly restrained stampede.

I don't know how—my eyes were closed—but Doug got us across town to the hospital by one. "Chipper" was definitely a thing of the past; I was now a screaming, out-of-control woman in labor. So much for candles and soothing music. So much for deep-breathing exercises and the family circle.

The nurses and midwife barely had time to rush me down the hall on a gurney and into the delivery room before Zachariah made his grand entrance—at 1:23 A.M.

Perhaps my birthing plan didn't unfold quite the way I had envisioned it. Zacky arrived not in dignity but in an unceremonious gush. Instead of candlelight and pan flutes, we had fluorescents and screams. But the result, my tiny, beautiful baby boy, turned the confusion and disorder of this destroyed delivery room to perfection itself.

Now it was the panic of our unceremonious dash to the hospital that faded away in the magical glow of that moment. No candlelight, no man-made music could have created this atmosphere of pure joy.

I hold Zacky to my breast and feel his warm breath on my flesh. His new skin is so tender and soft, softer than anything I have ever touched in the world. I'm sure it was only a few weeks ago that I held my first son this way and felt his rhythmic breathing. When I close my eyes and hold Zack's tiny hands in mine, they become his big brother's hands . . . hands I held as we strolled along the beach . . . hands I held as I walked him to his first day in school. Hands that caught baseballs I tossed. Hands that played in dough and clay. Hands that solemnly clasped as he recited his prayers on bended knee next to a race-car bed.

With Zack's head tucked under my chin, I cradle his tiny feet in my hand. A few weeks ago the nurse put ink on his newborn feet and made perfect little footprints on his birth certificate and in his baby book. They are so small that his baby booties fall off, and I have to wrap him in a receiving blanket so they won't get cold.

I hear the clump of large feet on our bare floors. Sonny strides in, with the same spring he's had since he learned to walk. I am sure it was just a few weeks ago that he was learning to crawl, then to walk, and then to run. I can still see the bumps and bruises he got racing haphazardly across the living room, tripping and falling, only to push himself up and try again. Perhaps I am wrong, perhaps it wasn't yesterday. I bought him new shoes for soccer last week—men's size thirteen.

Zack begins to stir and fuss and I know he's hungry again. As I cradle him in my arms and nurse him, I realize it wasn't yesterday but yesteryear that my firstborn was dependent upon me for his nourishment as well. Today he is becoming a man. My heart swells with pride as I watch the wonderful person he is becoming, but it also aches with sorrow to know he is no longer the little boy who once clung so tightly to Mom.

Because I have stood watching at the window of my children's lives I know how quickly the years fly away. I cradle Zacky just a little closer, trying to freeze this moment forever in time.

A CHILD'S BIRTH

You learn a lot about living when a child is born.

You learn that pain can overwhelm and overtake
and you wonder
how your own mother survived.

You clench your fists and tear the sheets
as life, entering life, tears your flesh.

And the moment you hold that tiny miracle,
your heart rips open in a way you never knew before.

Your flesh will heal in time.
You lie bleeding, not your flesh so much as your soul.

You know that every minute of every hour of every day
you will be consumed with love.
And fear is the unwelcome guest that will ride upon love's
    new wings.

You touch your now-empty belly and mourn the life you
    once had all to yourself.
You hold this life, naked flesh to naked flesh.
Nurse them to your breast,
rejoice that you can still provide what they need to
    survive . . .

You close your eyes and clutch their tiny fingers as they
    form to yours.
And in your heart you know

that one day they will not be yours to hold

and you feel the tearing of your soul go even deeper . . .

And again you wonder how your own mother survived.

How her sanity remained when her child was no more . . .

You learn a lot about living when a child is born . . .

Delilah

A Time to Die

’ve thought a lot about death over the years—more so now than in the past—probably because half my family has experienced it and the other half is left here to pick up the pieces and carry on. Or maybe it’s on my mind now more than before because of the gray eyebrows I keep plucking out, or the arthritis I feel in my left foot each morning.

Now and again, when my best friends get together, we have our “death rules” talk—you know, that discussion about what to do if something terrible happens. We cover the basics, of course, like organ donations and no artificial life support if hope is gone but breath is not . . . but we also talk about the other important rules . . . stuff like: no lacy-collared dresses on the deceased. A good friend of mine who always preferred sweatshirts and blue jeans to dresses or skirts was fitted by her well-meaning relatives with a lacy, frilly, collared dress for her funeral. I know if she could, she'd have ripped that foolish lace collar off right there in the casket and donned her jeans jacket and riding boots.

My friends and I make rules to cover stuff like the socks/no socks issue. Personally, I hate socks on my feet in bed. If I decide for some strange reason that socks might somehow help on a cold night, I'm uncomfortable all night. I can't ever get into a really good, deep sleep if I'm wearing socks in bed. But my friends Janey and Linda love to wear soft, warm socks to bed. So, we have agreed to honor one another's wishes if any one of us ever ends up incapacitated. Socks for them. No socks for me.

And there's the ever-important secret hairs code: if one of us develops one of those annoying wiry hairs that grows out of a mole on her chin, we have promised to pluck it out for our sick buddy before anyone notices.

Then there is the bedding problem. When I'm in bed I hate to have blankets touch my face. Especially fuzzy blankets. I like old, worn-out cotton sheets pulled up and over the blankets so only the sheet touches my face. And I have to have a feather pillow. A somewhat flat feather pillow. In an old cotton pillowcase. My grandma's pillowcases are the best. My husband likes lumpy foam pillows. And he pushes the sheets away.

If you are sick and dying in a hospital bed, will the nurses be concerned with these things, or will they focus on such trivia as blood sugar levels and whether or not your heart is beating?

To be honest, death doesn't scare me in the slightest. In fact, I'm actually looking forward to it. When I was a young person I was afraid of dying. I guess I always believed there was an up as well as a down, and that once you died you either got the express elevator to the top floor or not. I didn't think I was good enough to get to take the ride up—I expected to be roasting marshmallows for eternity. I didn't have a clue who God was, but I sure didn't want to die and not meet Him. Now I believe that though I'll never be good enough to take the up elevator, by my faith I get to spend eternity in heaven.

The Bible says, "No eye has seen, no ear has heard, no mind has conceived what God has prepared for those who love him." My ears have heard many wonderful sounds. My newborn babies' cries . . . water rushing over Niagara Falls . . . waves crashing on the rocky Oregon shore . . . flocks of birds singing in the morning as they gather around the backyard feeder.

And music. Music performed in summer parks by long-haired poets playing mandolins. Classically trained voices accompanied by ancient organs in steepled churches. A simple song, sung by my husband, as we dance in the living room cheek-to-cheek.

And my eyes . . . they've seen some pretty incredible sights.

Sunset on the Pacific . . . the Olympic Mountains painted a fiery orange . . . a bald eagle bathing in the cool waters of Lake Shasta . . . autumn foliage in New England . . . humpback whales singing off the coast of Massachusetts . . . killer whales breaching in Puget Sound . . . paintings by van Gogh . . . paintings by Monet . . . paintings by my children.

Yes, I've seen the glories of this world. So when I think about death, I get excited. I mean, if heaven is supposed to be better than the best this world has to offer, I can't wait!

It's getting there that frightens me. I've thought about this a lot, and as far as I can see, there aren't a lot of great ways to get from point A to point B. Life is good, heaven will be great . . . but getting there is going to be hell.

Basically, it appears to me that you have two choices, a quick surprise or a slow knowing. The quick surprise, like a car crash or an accidental drowning, used to appeal to me. Not a lot of suffering, no drawn-out hospital stays or painful, miserable treatments. Then I lost a few people that way and I saw how much business was left unfinished. Business like "I love you" that was never spoken. Relationships that were never healed. Business like letters and papers that had to be sifted through and read, books that had to be packed, personal stuff that had to be sorted.

I don't want someone going through my stuff if I suddenly die! I shudder to think what they might discover . . . do I want other people knowing that years after my baby was born I was still wearing maternity underwear? Or that my hair color came from Kmart?

The other choice—a slow, painful death from illness—doesn't appeal to me either. I watched folks I love die that way, and it was so hurtful to see them trying to protect me from the reality of their illnesses. I don't like hospitals. I don't like carrots that look like baby food. I don't like the thought of not being able to wipe my own butt.

Then again, if you're dying and you know you're dying, you can go to Victoria's Secret and buy fancy new underwear and leave it in your drawer for others to find when you're dead. They don't have to know it's three sizes too small. And you can destroy all those old journals you wrote while working through your issues on your path to emotional wellness. Heaven forbid my kids should read those.

Every time someone calls my show and tells me they have lost a loved one, I listen to hear how. I try to figure out if the pain was more or less intense because of the way the person died. I've talked with people who lost loved ones in house fires trying to save the lives of children inside. Did I hear any less agony in the voice of the firefighter's widow because he died a hero? Not that I could tell.

I've received thousands of calls from people who lost loved ones to cancer. Breast cancer. Brain cancer. Bone cancer. Blood cancer. Bowel cancer. I have heard from moms who lost babies to cancer. Children who have lost moms to cancer. Daughters who are grieving for their fathers, fathers who are grieving for their fathers because of cancer. I listen, trying to determine if spending time with the one they loved and saying good-bye made the pain any less. Not that I can tell.

I have watched footage of the floods in southern Africa, and famines that have taken the lives of thousands. I have wondered if being eaten alive by a shark is the most terrifying way to die, and then I've seen photos of children caught in the ravings of war, and I think perhaps that's the worst. I have tried to put myself in the position of those trapped in the Oklahoma City bombing, or in the massive earthquakes in South America, wondering: What is it like to be living, knowing you will die if no one comes to save you?

I have studied capital punishment, trying to figure out if one method is "better" than another. Throughout history humans have done some pretty amazing things to kill others. The cross, the lion's den, the guillotine, the noose, the firing squad, the electric chair, the gas chamber, the needle. A few of these are quick, but you still suffer, knowing death is coming.

So, I have determined that a nice, quiet heart attack in my sleep when I am ninety-five years old is the way I want to die. With my socks off. Sleeping under old cotton sheets. My head on a feather pillow. And no facial hairs.

I woke to the sound of the telephone ringing and groped around on the nightstand for it. Wiping the sleep from my eyes I managed to mumble, "Good morning, Mom," quietly, so as not to wake the sleeping baby next to me. I propped myself up on one arm and casually asked, "What time is Matt's plane arriving today?"

"It's not."

In less than an instant I had forgotten about being quiet for my infant son's sake. "What do you mean, it's not?"

"I didn't want to call you last night because we were sure there was just some misunderstanding, but . . . your brother's plane has disappeared." Her voice was so raw and hollow I thought for a moment someone else had suddenly taken the phone. "He and Anne haven't been heard from since yesterday morning."

I barely remember the hours that followed. In a tearful frenzy I threw on some clothes, grabbed my overnight bag, and started shoving stuff into it, hardly aware of what I was packing for Sonny and me. I called my two best friends in Oregon and told them that my brother and his wife were missing and I was on my way down.

Missing was all I could grasp. Missing I could handle—like the many nights I cried myself to sleep while my first husband was missing at the bars. Missing—like being disowned and missing from family functions. Missing wasn't final. Missing allowed for hope. I kept reassuring myself: They've landed in a farmer's field, or a clearing in the Oregon woods. We'll hear from them soon. They'll call or radio to say, We're OK, sorry to scare you.

I raced down the long stretch of highway from Seattle to Eugene, fighting Memorial Day traffic and stormy weather. The windshield wipers flailed at the downpour in vain. With my free hand I tried to wipe away my own personal downpour.

At that point in my life I had no faith, no relationship with God. And yet I found myself praying, pleading, begging some unknown Being to make everything all right as I drove on through the pouring rain.

Matt was the one with all the faith. He and his sweet wife, Anne, sang at churches, preached in churches, taught Sunday school for churches. My parents, the Lukes, had named him Matthew Mark Luke at birth—it was a tongue-in-cheek act without an ounce of devotion to those gospels. When he decided to be born again and was baptized, it was as if he'd slapped our family in the face. I wanted no association whatsoever with the right-wing fanatics I associated with the term "Christian." I felt, like the rest of my family, that Matt had been sucked into some sort of mind-control cult—that his decision to "get religion" had more to do with getting the blond he had fallen in love with and little to do with worshiping God. But Matt stuck with his new life, and after several years of dating, the blond became his wife. And now they were both missing, and I needed their God to help.

The nightmare continued for days. One of the volunteer search planes looking for them went down in the same terrible storm that had enveloped them. All three on board the search plane were killed. Day after day the rain fell. Day after day search efforts were stymied by thick clouds. My mother had a breakdown. Had it not been for the sweet baby I cradled, I would have broken down too.

I had left my hometown of Reedsport six years before, a hardheaded girl with a chip on her shoulder and a point to prove. I resented the small-town people and their small-town ways. I wanted to show the world I was better than those I left behind, breathing the putrid stench of their paper mill.

Now these same small-town people showed up in droves to help search for my brother and his wife. They came with food so my mother wouldn't have to cook. They came with money to help pay for the search. They came in four-by-fours and Jeeps, giving up their vacation days to comb the mountainsides. They came and sat in silence, just so we wouldn't be alone. Even the young Boy Scouts came, organizing search teams to beat the thick, tangled underbrush. The men and women who worked at the mill volunteered hundreds of hours roaming the same thick forests that they normally cut down. Together they searched. Together they prayed.

For seven years, we found no trace of Matt and Anne. When the wreckage was finally found, there were only a few bone fragments, Anne's wedding rings, and Matt's dog tags. It appeared that their plane had exploded on impact.

Seven years is a long time. For me it was a time of painful transformation. I had been running so hard since I left home— my brother's disappearance stopped me cold. I had been wasting so much energy being ambitious, angry, and self-centered. Now I looked about me and I felt love . . . from neighbors, childhood friends, and total strangers. Where did all this love come from? How could so much love exist in the hearts of these people that there was love to spare for my family and for me?

This was a love that came out of tragedy. It was a gift from my brother to all of us. And as the years of agony crawled on, day after day of uncertainty, my mind racing, desperate for some reason to hope that Matt and Anne could still be alive somewhere, gradually I saw that the source of that love was a God who was always there, giving us comfort, shoring up our courage, leading us toward acceptance and peace. In the midst of my despair at losing my brother, I found the God he worshiped. And through those terrible years, I learned what real love is.

Matt is gone, and I have accepted that I will not see him in this lifetime. But I'm looking forward to seeing him again in the next. We'll have a lot of catching up to do.

As painful as it is to lose a loved one, there is a strange, bittersweet joy when you feel the presence that person left behind. My listener Beth shared her experience in a letter she sent me.

When my grandma died, Delilah, I was devastated, knowing I would never be with her or even near her again. I held on to all her special possessions with care, especially her ladybug collection. She loved ladybugs and had tons of ladybug gadgets and decorations in her home. Nothing made me feel better, even when I looked through her things, remembering.

One day I was especially upset and so I drove to her grave site. I sat by her headstone and cried and talked to her about how I was feeling. Then I really lost it and started sobbing, yelling, "Why am I even here talking to you? This is a waste of time—you're not even here with me and I'm talking to you like you are."

I looked down at the ground, and I couldn't believe my eyes. On a single blade of grass sat a ladybug. I put my hand down and the ladybug crawled onto my finger and just sat for a few moments. A feeling of peace came over me and I took a cleansing breath of air. Then the ladybug scooted to the end of my finger, stuck her wings out, and flew up into the air. I know it was my grandma telling me she would always be with me.

My friend Janey—who is not only my producer but a part of my heart and my life—comes from a large family. I have never in my life seen the sort of commitment and solidarity that I have seen in her family. She is one of seven siblings, and they are all so close it is simply amazing. Her father, Bud, became like a father to me when I moved to the East Coast. Because my own father had disowned me years before, I had always longed for a father figure. Bud opened his huge arms wide and embraced me and my family. He was a mountain of a man with a twinkle in his eye and a dry sense of humor. When God called him home, Janey was able to be with him. Here is what she wrote about those last precious days.

His once brilliant silver hair lay, tired, atop his head. His gray-blue eyes worked hard to stay alert and in the moment. Sitting in his hospital bed, wrapped in blankets, this once colossal source of strength appeared childlike. At that moment he wanted only one thing: to get up and out of that bed. After some badgering on my part, a male nurse finally helped me get him safely into a wheelchair. He appeared to improve immediately. Upright, his face flashed with hope and pride.

We were off in an instant, rolling through the hospital corridors as fast as we could go. Several times we passed a great bay window that showed off a beautiful February afternoon. The winter sun seemed to be bathing everything in an extra soft and warm light. As we journeyed on, I could tell he was enjoying the movement and the air swirling around his face. So I pushed the chair even faster. He smiled, and suddenly I felt a little hope myself.

We must have covered several miles around the same corridor that day, laughing and greeting other patients and visitors as we repeatedly passed their rooms. We joked and reminisced about family members and events. Though it was hard for him, he bravely laid down his pain and fear and took this time to celebrate life with me. I could tell he was getting tired but he did not want to go back to bed yet. Eventually we found ourselves stopped at the great bay window, which provided a generous view of the now late afternoon.

We giggled together as we watched an old woman trying to parallel-park. "Women drivers," he said in his playful way. Standing there behind his chair, I found myself laughing out loud. Through the laughter a sudden flood of tears ran down my face and I realized what the word "bittersweet" means. I leaned down to hug him. His voice was almost a whisper, but he managed to say, "I love you all so much. I feel like the luckiest man in the world. My kids are so good to me." As these words fell on my ears I felt more love for this man than I had ever felt before. Here he was facing the most difficult challenge a person ever can—his death. Instead of focusing on that, he was doing what he always did, putting his children first.

As I hugged him close, all I could think of was the endless hours he put in at work. The necessities he always provided. The faith he lived by and shared, the family movies he so enjoyed making. The way he could fix anything, and I do mean *anything*. The gallons of milk he brought home every night. The crazy ice cream he would buy—like Banana Peel Special—just because it was on sale.

The Sunday breakfasts he cooked, the family vacations, and those treasured late-afternoon trips to the beach. There were so many times—endless hours of laughter, fun, and memories to last a lifetime. But mostly I thought of the way he made me feel safe, like no one else on this earth ever could or ever will again.

I could say nothing. I struggled to catch my breath. There was so much I wanted to tell him, so much I wanted to say, so much I wanted him to understand. But I knew at that moment neither of our hearts could take it. This moment was a gift from God, a gift to be felt and shared and cherished. While we stared out of that wonderful window I simply said, "Daddy, I love you."

The glorious winter sun dipped in a crimson sky, and I knew it meant more than just another end to an ordinary day. The sun was setting on our earthly time together. It was a rare and precious moment, our chance to say farewell.

Jane

Death is something you think is for the old, the aged, the great-grandparents, but this is not always the case. Many of us lose loved ones when we are still virtually children. Such was the case with my listener Leslie.

I was ten when I first met Karen. I had been separated from my family and was starting over in a new town. At the time I was a timid, lonely, and reserved little girl who could use a good friend. I remember it like it was yesterday. Karen came bouncing up to me with her beautiful smile and said, "Hi, I like your hat. You wanna hang out with me?" She was the only person in the whole school who welcomed me. I was grateful.

In school, Karen and I were inseparable. We always shared a locker, joined the same school clubs, attended the same functions. We were on the same wavelength. By the time we reached adolescence, our differences had emerged. Karen was the outrageous, rebellious, "I'll do anything" type. I was the commonsense, grounded, "Let's not get in trouble" type. As you can imagine, Karen got me into quite a few predicaments: school skippings, missed curfews, parties, boys, alcohol, and drugs. She would always find a way to get us into trouble and I would always have to find the way out.

She lived on the edge and I clung to the opposite side. Our willingness and ability to meet in the middle somehow kept me sane and her alive!

In college, Karen and I were dorm roommates. College was a big adjustment: tough courses, stuffy professors, and lots of parties. Our lives were full. I guess that's why it took me so long to notice the change in Karen's behavior. She started sleeping all the time. I finally urged her to see a doctor. We thought she was just run-down and needed to take better care of herself. We never expected to hear the dreaded word. Cancer.

The following months were a nightmare, filled with surgeries, chemotherapy, feelings of hope, then hopelessness. She'd appear to be getting better, then we'd get more bad news. Through it all, Karen's courage and relentless fight were amazing. We had long talks about our lives and dreams, and our futures.

But there was no happy ending. Karen died. It's been twelve years now and it's still a shock. I think about all the things she's missed that I wanted to share with her, like the birth of my son. She would have been his godmother. She was always there for me when no one else was, and I'll never forget her for that. She taught me many things. Don't let life pass you by, never be afraid to take a chance. I only wish we'd had more time.

I believe God has a plan for everyone. I think we can sometimes modify the plan, but some things are inevitable. That's how I make sense of the situation. This is what brings me comfort and peace. You know, even though the end was rough, almost unbearable at times, I wouldn't exchange my friendship with Karen for anything in the world. I know she's still with me. I constantly feel her presence.

It had been several days since Mom had last spoken. Her head was twisted painfully to one side, but any attempts to shift her into a more comfortable position were met with a terrible wince on her already contorted face. Her bright green eyes were closed and her once strong hands lay limp at her sides. We took turns sitting with her, talking to her, waiting for the inevitable, yet praying for a miracle. The nurses told us it was only a matter of time before the raspy breathing would be silenced. Still, I clung to a thread of faith.

I had been sleeping on a makeshift bed in the family room with her, waking every few hours to make sure she was comfortable, to swab her mouth with cool water—and to nurse my infant daughter. It was strange, caring for them both at the same time.

My mother and I had a classic relationship. We loved each other fiercely, but our headstrong personalities clashed at every crossing. She had built her world around being our mom, and when we grew up, she couldn't let go.

Now, watching her, I felt so tied to her I thought my own heart also might stop. If it hadn't been for Shaylah, I don't know how I would have survived the week. Just when I thought I could take no more grief, Shaylah would crawl up to me, thrust her chubby hands upward, and beg to be held. Tightly I clutched her to my breast as she nursed, gently I cradled her next to me when I slept. Holding Shaylah's tiny hand, a miniature version of mine and Mom's, I knew there was nothing I wouldn't do to protect this gift God had given me. Perhaps because she is so like me, I want to shelter her from making all my bad mistakes. Suddenly I understood my mother's inability to let go of her children.

The sun filtered through the heavy curtains and I opened my eyes to check on Mom. Her breathing was more labored, but her green eyes were wide open. She was blinking as if to adjust to the morning light. Gently I tried to crawl out of my bed without waking Shay.

"Mom, if you can hear me, let me know," I said. She looked at me and blinked. I told her how much we all loved her, and how much God loved her, too. Through my stinging tears, I told her not to be afraid, that God and her son and her mother were waiting for her. She blinked again, and gently squeezed my hand. Her friend Carlile came into the room and we prayed together.

Shaylah woke up and wanted to nurse. I was trying to keep her quiet as I focused my attention on Mom. "Not now, honey, in a minute," I said, but Shaylah only insisted in a louder voice.

Then Mom tapped my hand with her index finger and shifted her eyes to Shaylah and back to me. Her command was obvious, even as death called her name. I let go of her hand for a moment, scooped Shaylah up, and sat down again next to Mom. Shay quieted as she began to nurse, and as I held her with my left arm I held Mom's hand in my right. Shay reached out and wrapped her fingers tightly around her grandma's fingers. I could see Mom's green eyes soften as she gazed at her granddaughter. And then she breathed no more.

The circle of life was complete.

You learn a lot about living,
watching someone die . . .
You learn that life isn't fair
and death doesn't care
and suffering visits us all.

You try to ease the pain,
to stop the torrent of rain

that floods your heart and eyes.
You turn your face away,
afraid they'll see how much you hurt
and try to fix it for you . . .

You learn that gifts don't really matter
    and money matters less.
You'd give it all back,
everything you've ever owned,
just to make her whole again.
You stroke her face,
you stroke her hands and talk of happy times . . .
Of walks in parks and camping trips,
of water dancing over rocks
and Christmas mornings brightly wrapped . . .
You talk of bike rides and snowball fights
    and picnics in the sun.

And when you can talk no more
    you sit and pray and argue
and beg and plead with the Giver of Life.
One more month, or week, or day,
you plead in sobs choked with fear.
Then beg.
Take her home, because you can't bear
    to watch her suffer.

Actually, you can't bear to watch her suffer,
knowing she's watching you.

When hair is gone, and breath is short
and nights are long and hope has faded like the flowers
by her bed, you learn that only love remains.

You learn a lot about living, in watching someone die . . .

Delilah

A Time to Plant

By the time I decided that diet pills and abusive men might not be real good hobbies to hang on to and gardening might be a bit healthier for my body as well as my soul, I was too late. Too late to gather wisdom from my green-thumbed grandma McGowne; she had already gone to tend her posies in that great garden in the sky. My mother knew the difference between a fig tree and a pear tree, but she wasn't well versed in which perennials loved shade and which molded away without full sunlight. Heaven forbid I should pick up a book and read, or join a horticulture society. No, most of what I learned came via trial and error. Mostly error.

I bought my first house when I was only twenty-two years old, a tiny little cottage the real estate agent called a fixer-upper, which is, I discovered, a quaint term for a shack that's falling down about your ears. Since I couldn't stand to look at the peeling wallpaper or the bright green linoleum, I wandered outside and focused instead on the ancient camellia in the front of the little house, with its bright pink blooms. I also found a delightful apple tree in the backyard, bearing three varieties of sweet fruit. It was probably fifty years old, lovingly grafted by someone years before I was born.

I dug flower beds to line the little path leading to the house and planted daffodils I found at the grocery store in little round pots. Little did I know they were meant to remain in little round pots. No one told me (maybe I should have asked) that you can't transplant daffodils once they've bloomed. So there I was, with two lovely brown patches of freshly dug dirt and forty or fifty bright yellow daffodils . . . prone, sprawling, as if slain in their prime. I watered them. I thought, Tomorrow they'll spring back up and be lovely . . . Not. So I snipped the wilted blooms and started over with small white daisies, purple pansies, and cornflowers. Within a few weeks my efforts began to pay off, and the front walk (if nothing else) looked quite fetching.

I bought a little Italian plum tree the day after the house

closed and planted it in the corner of the front yard; it was about four feet tall and had two branches. I picked it out because it reminded me of the Charlie Brown Christmas tree. Somewhere I have a picture of that tiny tree the day I planted it—so filled with hope and joy was I, with my little shack, my new marriage, my hopes for the future . . .

Since that time, I've moved many times, lost much, and found more. But everywhere I've been, I've found or made a garden. Each home I settled in, I made friends with neighbors who were passionate about gardening, and they shared their wisdom—and some of their favorite plants—with me. Each move I made, I pulled up starts of all my favorite flowers and took them with me. To me they aren't just flowers that grow and bloom. They're reminders of friends and family I love, and the times we've had together. I've seen scores of plants—and people—grow and blossom in gardens. My listeners and friends have told me of many more.

Gently I cup the tiny, tender petals in my hands. Gazing at their delicate beauty, I lose myself among the blossoms . . . soft, sweet, and innocent. How many springs had I watched as my grandma McGowne's shears sought out vines damaged by winter's jealous malice? How many summer mornings had I found her dragging the garden hose to soak the ground beneath tender new growth?

How many of her pot roast dinners were more complete because the centerpiece was a milk-glass vase overflowing with wild rose blossoms? How many freckle-faced dreamers had dined with kings and queens upon a table festooned with these miniature flowers? How many of her friends, perhaps ill and abed, were cheered by a fresh-cut bouquet of pink, wrapped in a wet toweling?

Thousands of blossoms blanket the big bush next to Grandma's drive each year. From my vantage point on the front porch swing, they seem a huge, soft explosion of light pink froth bathed in summer's long twilight. I gaze at the little cluster of flowers in my hand and realize I have picked more than flowers . . . and I let the memories come.

For thirteen years she fought on against disease, proving the doctors wrong. She lost her soft, dark hair. Lost her breasts. Lost her full, round figure. Lost her strength to knead her homemade yeast rolls. Lost the energy to walk to the mailbox at the end of the country road. But she never lost her courage. Or her gentle smile. Or her wild, pink roses. They grew strong even as she grew weak, and never seemed to fade. Heartier than the aloof tea roses she also loved, these little wild ones are still my favorites. My grandmother may be gone, but her roses live on. In their presence, I am in hers. I have heard it said, "God gives us memories that we might have roses in December." I have plenty of both, beautiful roses and beautiful memories.

Every day we plant something, whether we know it or not. And if we tend it well, it will grow, somewhere, someday. My listener Patrina is a gardener who planted a dream and didn't even know it. This is her story.

*W*hen I first met Garry I was a junior in high school. I've always loved roses, and in one of my classes I had drawn up plans for a rose garden. I showed the plan to Garry. We got married a year later, and I completely forgot about my rose garden. We've been married for almost nineteen years. I love my husband dearly, but he has a terrible memory—sometimes I wonder if he's listening when I talk to him.

Well, to my complete surprise, for Valentine's Day four years ago Garry planted me a rose garden. He told me that he remembered how excited I was when I showed him the plans I had drawn up, and he wanted to make my childhood dream come true. We had never been anywhere he could do this before, but now we owned our own home. The rose garden has grown and flourished, and every summer the sweet smell of roses is everywhere.

Some days Garry will even bring me a rose from the garden just to make sure I still know how much he loves me. He may not have a very good memory for the everyday stuff, but he sure remembers my dreams.

Garry isn't always home. He's in the navy. He'll be gone this Valentine's Day and I miss him so much. But every time I look out my windows I can see proof of his love, growing in my yard.

An insightful newspaper editor named Hodding Carter Jr. wrote, "There are only two lasting bequests we can give our children. One is roots. The other is wings." I saw this quote on a plaque in the living room of a neighbor I baby-sat for as a teenager.

Thank goodness my children haven't reached an age to be flying away from the nest yet, but I try my best to give them roots. Which is somewhat difficult, given that we've moved more than half a dozen times these past few years . . . given that the six children in our house have two different biological mothers and four different biological fathers. (You need to have passed Algebra 1 to figure out that equation.) I can't give my adopted ones the "Here's your family tree" kind of roots. I can't tell them where their forefathers came from or how they got where they are today. But I can give them the roots of traditions, values, and faith in the family God has created.

I love to garden. It has become one of my passions the past ten years or so. Gardening is a lot like parenting. You have to carefully tend the soil, making sure it is rich and fertile. You have to know when to plant and when to prune. You have to know which season is the right season to dig up a bulb, and which is the right season to separate the roots of an overgrown perennial. You have to keep a close eye on the weeds, pulling them up as soon as they appear, before they sprout and take over and destroy all you've worked so hard to cultivate. And the blossoms . . . oh, the glorious, wonderful flowers that open when you love and care for them. Just like children—each one different, each one spectacular.

A few years ago our family made another of its many moves. We packed up our household goods and called a moving company. The movers asked us where we wanted the goods shipped. Because we weren't sure where we were moving yet, we didn't know the answer, so we told them to put everything in storage. This meant all the plants I had dug out of my garden would die in a cold, sunless storage unit somewhere. So rather than ship my precious plants, I put the pots in my mother-in-law's yard, and she babysat them for me.

When we finally knew we were moving from the East to

the West Coast, my husband packed the back of our van with dozens of pots and two huge coolers filled to the brim with plants, and he drove them three thousand miles across the country. Just he and a hamster named Sam. The rest of us flew. Our trip took a few hours; his took twelve days. For my plants. That's love.

Soon we moved from a tiny little house to a much bigger one. That house was soon too small (one bathroom, eight people . . . not good), and a year ago we moved again to an even larger house. Each time we move, there are plants that must be moved as well—Grandma's pink rosebush, a start I got years ago; the Japanese iris my neighbor in Boston gave me; and the hostas my neighbor in Philly shared. Some people keep scrapbooks to remind them of the people and places they love. I keep living flowers.

My yard is looking a little rough this year. The garden has taken a backseat to my infant son's needs. But once he discovers the joys of dirt, this will change. As he grows, I'm hoping that like his sister Shay, Zacky will love the garden and that he'll see and be nurtured by its beauty.

Her body language spoke volumes. She stood there, her arms firmly crossed, her feet squarely planted. When she walked she dug her hands deep into her pockets, or balled them into half fists at her side. Then, once in a while, she would laugh and the invisible walls would recede, but only for a few moments. When we became friends, she had been drinking for over fifteen years. But behind the tough-girl exterior was a tender heart, waiting to bloom.

Ruth calls herself a Philly girl. She had, without question, seen the darker streets of Philadelphia. Given up for adoption at birth, she was raised by parents who resided at opposite ends of the spectrum. Her mother was a sweet, simple woman who loved to cook and can fresh fruits and sing silly songs to her two adopted children. Her father was a wealthy, well-educated alcoholic who was sure he knew and understood everything and everyone. There was only one way to do things—his way. When these two divorced, the brother and sister became pawns in their bitter battle. Ruthie's mother was left with nothing but a beanbag chair and a broken heart. Her simple nature and her fears kept her from picking up the pieces and going on.

Somehow, the father won custody of the two children, but custody to him didn't mean spending time with them. He would hand his eleven-year-old daughter $50 and tell her to have a good weekend, and jet off to visit his new girlfriend in Canada. He seemed to despise Ruth as much as he adored his son. He told her she was too stupid to succeed at anything. Unfortunately, she believed him.

By the time she was a young teen she was running with a fast crowd. She searched for love, and older men used her. Drugs and alcohol filled the void left by her broken family.

The first time she called my show, she was drunk. I said, "Pour out the booze and we'll talk." When I came back to the phone a few minutes later she reported the booze was gone. "Now, go dump the Baileys and the Kahlua," I said.

"How did you know?" she said.

Ruth knew she had a problem, and she had reached a point in her life where she was really, truly ready to change. I shared my faith with her and told her that God would see her through. She checked into rehab and got the drugs and alcohol out of her system.

The first few months of her sobriety were difficult, but she attended her meetings and talked to her sponsor. We became close. Then I got laid off and had to move out of state. Our circle of friends dispersed and she went back to hanging out with her partying buddies. Before long she was back on the streets, hitting the bottle. She called in tears one day. "I need help. I can't do this by myself." So she left her successful career, left her apartment and her party buddies, and moved in with my family. We surrounded her with love. We held her shaking hands while she detoxed. I brought her to AA meetings. We took her to the store when she was too sick to drive. I cooked her meals to nourish her body, read her books to nourish her soul. Though the drugs and alcohol were gone from her system in a few weeks, the poison of anger at the betrayal she had experienced remained.

Meanwhile, my own life was turned upside down by the death of my mother and the loss of yet another job. It had been a difficult, painful winter. My heart was broken, my marriage was strained, my bills were piling up, my baby was teething, and I hadn't slept in weeks.

I went outside and started working in my garden. After a few hours in the dirt, I felt the tension melt away and joy began to flood back in. I always feel close to God when I'm working in the soil, digging and planting and pruning. I stood and stretched my back, and Ruth came and stood beside me. She started asking questions about the flowers I was tending, the vegetable garden I was planning. The next day she asked if she could go with me to the nursery when I went to pick up more plant starts and seeds. I was surprised she was so interested; she had always seemed like such a city girl. At the hardware store she picked out a pair of gloves and some garden tools of her own. When we got home, she went right to work.

She took on a slope outside my kitchen window as her first project. Within a few days we had it dug up, turned over, and ready for a rock wall. Working together, with my husband, Doug, helping, we carried the stones for the wall. Then we planted perennials, laid a rock path, and set up a birdbath. Before long she was getting up in the morning much earlier than me. I would find her coffee cup in the sink, and she'd be working in the garden.

I had planted some lovely pansies in the front of the ancient house, just randomly scattered the plants about. One day I came home after an exhausting week at my new job to find them dug up and replanted by color and variety. She had painted a scene with the flowers, their delicate faces smiling in the sun.

Ruth soon took over a huge section of the yard. She planted several new rosebushes in my rose garden, and lined the edges with bright purple lobelia. Then she started on the marigold section, as we called it. Bright yellow sunflowers, golden black-eyed Susans, and dozens and dozens and dozens of fiery marigolds. Every day she watered each plant and trimmed back the dead leaves.

Now, I noticed, something else was happening. The garden wasn't enough for her—she began to take care of *me*! She would sit with my son and help him with his math. She bounced my baby girl for hours, trying to get her to sleep so I could rest. She shared her professional experience with my husband, who was trying to get a new business off the ground. She did my dishes and helped with the laundry. She got two jobs and gave nearly every dime she earned to help me with our bills. When she had moved in, it was so we could help her. Now Ruthie was trying to help me.

I watched in amazement as beautiful things grew and blossomed. Not just roses and marigolds, but my friend's soul. Her face softened and she began to let her hands remain at her side, relaxed—no longer clenched for a fight. As she spent hours pulling dandelions and dock weeds out of the garden, God was pulling the weeds of anger and resentment from her heart. As she nurtured each and every plant, God was nurturing a soul that had been abandoned for most of its life. As she poured herself into tending the garden, God poured Himself into the garden of her heart.

I love sunflowers—the way their cheery faces peer down from on high and seem to smile and wave as you walk by. My grandma McGowne always planted hundreds of them along the edge of her huge garden, and in summer and late fall they stood like sentinels watching over the rows of ripening tomatoes and green beans and stalks of corn. After they bloomed she would cut them down and hang the huge heads in the rafters of the fish shack—a little outbuilding next to her house that overlooked the Allegheny River. The fish shack was warm and cozy, heated by an old black potbellied woodstove. Grandpa Mac would cut and stack the wood and keep a nice fire going while he and his cronies sat and caught the huge fish that were abundant then in the river. The sunflowers would dry and we'd have buckets of seeds to feed the birds over the winter months.

Today Grandma is gone to be with God. The sunflowers are gone, the fish are no longer plentiful. Even the wild songbirds have all but disappeared. My grandpa lives alone, a solitary, stubborn old man on the river.

But every summer I plant sunflowers, no matter where I live. They remind me to look up and be cheerful. They remind me of my grandparents and the little piece of heaven up the river. Over the years I've gotten a little creative, mixing the traditional tall golden yellow sunflowers that Grandma grew with other varieties: the smaller burnished red ones, exotic amber gold ones, and fluffy "teddy bear" sunflowers. This year I planted a couple of rows along the fence in our backyard so I could look at them as I stood at the kitchen window doing dishes.

They grew quickly and developed huge, brightly colored blossoms. Brilliant yellow faces smiled at me when I got up in the morning, and the smaller, red ones would dance in the wind. One morning I looked out and noticed a few of the taller sunflower stalks broken in half, the blooms almost touching the ground. I assumed the weight of their seeds had pulled them down, so I went out and tied them to the fence with twine.

A few days later I discovered more of my beautiful sunflowers bent double, as if they had bad stomachaches. Since they had been secured to the fence, I decided my boys must have been playing soccer in the yard and kicked the ball into the flowers. I reprimanded Sonny and our new foster son, Manny, and asked them to be more careful. "We didn't break your flowers, Mom," they insisted. I gave them that suspicious "mom look" and went about my gardening . . .

The next morning I got up earlier than usual because the boys were back in school. I looked out the kitchen window just in time to see a huge, fat gray squirrel run up the fence, jump full force on the face of a bright yellow sunflower, and ride it to the ground, where he proceeded to pull out handfuls of seeds and stuff them into his fat cheeks. He disappeared for a few minutes and then returned. Instead of attacking the already wounded sunflower, he chose another one along the fence and assumed the attack position. He flew through the air, but he had miscalculated. The sunflower he decided to pounce upon was one of the smaller, burnt red ones, with a much weaker stem. Instead of lowering him gracefully to the ground, it snapped in half and he went tumbling into the soft earth below.

I laughed as I watched him destroy my flowers, enjoying every minute . . . as beautiful as the sunflowers were when they held their colorful heads high, they didn't bring me nearly the pleasure as when they were doing what God had designed them to do—provide seeds for the wild creatures that add such beauty to our lives.

And then I humbly apologized to my boys.

A garden is a magical place to spend time with people you love. Gardening is also a neutral activity, a pure and natural act of love that yields inspiring results. Kristin wrote me a note about just such an experience.

I just spent the most precious weekend with my grandmother, who is in her eighties. I am her oldest granddaughter and I'm single.

She just came to visit me in my first home, which I recently bought. We had plans for her to teach me to plant a vegetable garden, but it was pouring down rain. At first we were really disappointed, but we decided that God sent the rain for a reason. Determined not to just waste our day, we went and bought flowers to plant.

When we got back, we decided to brave the weather and plant the flowers anyway. We had so much fun. We got muddy and laughed so much. Our day together turned out to be wonderful in spite of the weather. The next day we awoke to a beautiful spring day and we were able to plant our vegetables.

I know that no matter what life has in store for us, I'll never forget this warm and touching time I spent with my grandmother.

It was the longest I had been away from home, almost a month. I was a counselor at Girl Scout camp. I was fifteen, and happy to be away from my strict father, but I missed my mother terribly.

The last week at camp, I was a tangle of emotions—I felt sadness at leaving newfound friends, a deep ache leaving the forest, and these were mixed with eagerness to see Mom and my brother and sisters. I was surprised when, instead of Mom, Grandma McGowne arrived to pick me up. She told me Mom had been sick and we would go to her house for a while— Mom would come get me in a few days.

Bewildered, I put my backpack and sleeping bag in the car, then ran back to my cabin for one final treasure. On one of my hikes, I had tenderly dug up two beautiful maidenhair ferns. It was not an easy task—their tough, thin roots prefer to wrap around rock and moss rather than sink down into loose soil.

Now I carried the coffee can I had put them in to the car, walking softly and watching every step.

The forests of the Oregon coast are a wonderland. Tall Douglas fir trees that reach to the sky form a canopy of evergreen boughs high in the air. The forest floor is a rich, damp tangle of Oregon grape, huckleberry, sword fern, and bracken. They're lovely and lush, but these are common plants, plentiful in the forest.

Hidden along the rocky banks of a mountain stream you can find the most delicate of all ferns—the maidenhair. Its lacy fronds look like gentle fingers dangling in the cold water. I couldn't wait to see Mom's face when I gave her these forest treasures.

I was shocked when she arrived at Grandma's. Mom was at least twenty pounds thinner than when I had left, less than a month before, and as pale as a ghost. I hadn't known it, but while I was away at camp she had nearly died during a fairly routine surgery procedure. She assured me she was fine now, but my relief was tinged with fear.

Twenty years later, I pushed Mom in a wheelchair across her backyard. The doctors had given her only a few weeks more to live. This time the enemy was cancer; there was nothing more they could do. After all the pain and the bleakness of the hospital, she wanted to sit in the warmth of her garden. We stopped before the same gentle maidenhair ferns I had brought her that still graced the corner of her yard. She could no longer speak clearly, but she pointed to the ferns and, reaching back to that distant time for my childhood nickname, whispered, "Remember, Sis?"

I remember, Mom. I remember.

A Time to Pull Up What Is Planted

We sat on Naugahyde kitchen chairs in the hot, stuffy attic, my sister and I. The mass of boxes and bags before us was daunting, but we knew we had to sort and sift through them, and time was running short. We had infants to care for and families that needed our attention. So we set about our task with grim determination. I was beginning to realize that I come by my pack-rat tendencies honestly.

It wasn't just our late mother's stuff that we had to sort through. The family home had become a sort of museum, a warehouse of our dead relatives' personal effects. First my brother and his wife had disappeared, and after five years the military had released their belongings to my family. Mom had meant to sort through all of Matt's boxes, but she had been so busy with life changes and traumas, she hadn't had a chance.

And then Grandma died. Mom got quite a lot of her clothes, antiques, and family heirlooms. These too were boxed and stored in the attic, to be sorted through "one day."

And then Dad died. His tools, drafting board, guitars, Avon cologne bottle collection, five thousand pounds of welding rods, three ancient boats, four clam shovels, six crab traps, fifteen broken wristwatches, a drilled-out three-ton safe, and various and sundry items were left to be assessed, sorted, and distributed.

Mom and Dad both became rather eccentric in their collecting and storing habits in their later years. We found at least four garbage bags full of packing peanuts in the attic. We found bolts and bolts of fabric Mom had purchased from the five-and-dime when we were children. It was homely material back in the sixties and it was homelier now. Dad spent the last twenty years of his life going to government auctions, bidding on everything from used police cars to outdated adding machines. He bought a flatbed-truck load of welding rods during one of his sprees, sixty used calculators at another.

We had tried to figure out some logical way to hold on to the family house and all of its weird collectibles, and all its bittersweet memories. We discussed keeping it as a summer home, since it was so near the ocean. But we lived so far away it would fall to ruin sitting empty all winter long. We discussed renting it to a friend, but that wasn't a practical option either. After a lot of tears and a lot of discussions, the three of us who remained knew we had to let it go.

We sorted, we packed, we laughed, and we cried. We found our mother's appendix in a bottle of formaldehyde, taken out when she was eleven. We found my brother's model airplane collection, complete with a replica of the plane he died in, built when he was just a child. We found every note, every card, every paper we had ever colored, drawn, or stapled while we were growing up. We found our dog's collar, complete with the tags issued when we got her in 1964. We found my sister's diary, filled with colorful words and hysterical ramblings from her thirteen-year-old point of view.

It was so very difficult to have an estate sale, to watch complete strangers rummaging through our memories, haggling over the price of a glass pitcher. How could they know that pitcher had held gallons of Kool-Aid, made by chubby hands for sale in a roadside stand? Ziploc sandwich bags contained baubles and beads, hundreds of pieces of my mother's tacky costume jewelry.

Petite women wearing size six clothes laughed at the huge collection of size twelve women's shoes for sale. They had no way of knowing my mom had worn men's shoes as a child because her folks couldn't find any big enough to fit her feet.

They didn't have a clue what it was like to be over six feet tall and horribly self-conscious about your size when you were only twelve years old. Their jokes were innocent enough, but they stung my grieving heart.

We saved those things we just couldn't bear to part with, like Dad's Martin guitar and Mom's milk-glass collection. We took starts from our favorite plants and flowers in the yard. We took cuttings from the fig tree in the back, the yellow rose-bush at the side of the house. We took pictures of our old bed-room. We took our time as we packed up the mementos, and then we closed the door and said good-bye to our little house on the hill. But we took our memories with us.

Change can be scary, whether it's moving to a new home or ending a relationship. But the rewards always outweigh the fear, and if you take charge of the transition, as my listener Rosemarie and her family did, change can become an unfor-gettable adventure.

*J*ust over two years ago my husband gave us a priceless gift of time—we sold our business and our home and bought a twenty-seven-foot RV. With no agenda and no timetable, we pulled up roots and took off to show our children this incred-ible country—Jason, thirteen; Kevin, eleven; and my baby,

Amanda Marie, nicknamed Amy, who was almost six. For twenty-one months we traveled, and every day was a new adventure. We saw all the major national parks, of course, and they were truly fantastic. And we found the smaller, out-of-the-way places were what we really loved to discover.

And the people! We spoke with lingcod fishermen, lumberjacks, gold prospectors, lobstermen, ostrich farmers, glassblowers, ferryboat pilots—the list is practically endless.

It wasn't always fun—we "experienced" Haight Ashbury, got lost in the Rockies, blew a tire in the Georgia backwoods (ever try jacking up an RV?), spent a night in a New Jersey ghetto, got caught between two sides in a riot. No, it wasn't always wonderful, but that, too, is the America we wanted our children to understand.

The best thing about this incredible trip, though, wasn't climbing the Statue of Liberty or descending into Carlsbad Caverns or exploring a tide pool. The best thing about this trip was having time. Time to consider how incredible the journey of Lewis and Clark really was. Time to sit on a beach strewn with giant trees washed up in Pacific storms. Time to rediscover the man I married and take another look at those dreams I had put on the shelf. Time to laugh and play with my little ones before they fly away.

I learned some very important things from this "escape from reality." I learned that the only way to get back up from the bottom of a deep canyon—on a trail or in life—is to keep putting one foot in front of the other. I learned that you usually take a path only once, so you'd better stop often and enjoy the view. I've learned that the people I thought I knew well have many surprising talents to share, if only I give them some time. But most of all I learned that there really is enough time. God gave me exactly the right amount—I just need to be a little bit wiser in how I spend it.

My sister knew I was moving away before I had a chance to tell her. I heard her sigh on the airport phone. I had just gotten off the plane from Boston and called her for a ride. As we hung up, it dawned on me that I hadn't known I was moving myself—not until the end of that conversation with the stranger on the plane.

He was as nondescript as the upholstery on the too-small seats, but pleasant, with a kind, fleshy face. He was almost giddy with excitement as he rambled on about his new job and the opportunities waiting for him in my hometown. I was too exhausted to respond much, but I enjoyed listening to the plans he and his family had made for their move. He had boarded the plane during a stopover in Dallas; I was halfway home from my trip to Boston. He was from upstate New York, he explained, and very happy to be leaving the heat of Texas, happy about the possibilities that lay ahead in Seattle.

I closed my eyes and tried to make sense of the past forty-eight hours. I had returned from a Memorial Day camping trip in the mountains with my son to find an urgent message on my answering machine. I returned the call and a few hours later I was boarding a red-eye flight clear across the country to a city I had never seen before. I had called my sister and asked if she would mind keeping Sonny for two days. When she heard why, she agreed, but her voice was heavy with sadness.

I was met at Logan Airport by an associate, George, and a limousine. I didn't even have time to change out of my jeans and sweater. In Seattle the air had been warm and sweet, but the Boston heat and humidity were stifling; I felt drenched with sweat the moment I stepped out of the luxurious car. We rushed to a meeting with a large man named Jim. Jim was from Texas; he had both the drawl and the cowboy boots.

They cut to the chase and offered me a job earning more money than I had ever dreamed of back in Seattle. They wanted me to start immediately, and had the limo driver show me some of the most beautiful neighborhoods I had ever seen in my life to convince me to move. Possibilities of a national radio show were spoken of, and creative freedom was offered. I was so unhappy and miserable at my job in Seattle, working for people who felt they knew best how I should be me, people who broke promises.

But my home, my heart, and my family were all in the West. I had moved from my tiny first home to a big old house two years earlier. I had hoped to raise my son there, spend my life tending its huge garden and painting pictures of its ancient fruit trees. I knew every inch of the wooded park down the hill, and I knew every side street in the city that had been home for almost a decade. I knew Carol at my bank and Paul at my grocery store. I knew which dry cleaner would have my blazer back in a day, which thrift shops held treasures.

Most of all, I had my sister and her family less than a mile away. As children we had fought nearly every day—as adults we talked and laughed together every day. DeAnna and her husband, Johnny, watched my son at night when I was at work, and kept him overnight every Friday so I could have Saturday mornings to myself. She knew how to fix Sonny's "pang-kakes" just the way he liked them, with the "see-rup" on the side so it didn't touch. She knew how to fix deviled eggs the best way—the filling piped into the egg halves, not just scooped in with a spoon the way his mom did it. She was more than his aunt, she was his Other-Mother, and Johnny was the only male role model in Sonny's life—his father had moved out of state.

We shopped together, my sister and I, sewed curtains together, laughed and cried together. When I bought my big house, she and Johnny spent hundreds of hours scraping and painting it for me, getting it ready for us to live in. She had grown from my little sister to my best friend. It would be very hard to say good-bye.

I listened to the man next to me on the plane talk about packing boxes and finding a school for his two young children. He said, "I'm not sure where we'll be living," and suddenly I said, "Are you looking for a house to rent?"

"Why, do you have one?" he asked.

"Maybe. I'm going to take my son and move to Boston," I said, surprised at the words leaving my mouth. Until that moment I had not decided to stay or go.

And now I stood in the crowded, noisy airport, calling to let Anna know I was back home. She was half asleep when she answered, but she could tell I had made up my mind. When they arrived at the airport to pick me up, her eyes were swollen and red, as were mine. The three years my sister and I had lived in the same neighborhood were coming to a close, and I felt torn. But my marriage had crumbled, my career had hit a dead end, and it was time to move on. It was time to pull up roots and go where God was leading me.

The current is swift,
the rushing water refreshingly cool.
But I hide
in my little hole,

my cove of comfort,

clinging to familiar vines of safety,

hanging on

to that which I've come to love.

Yet the rushing water

beckons me,

whispering my name,

inviting,

impatient,

insisting,

urging me

to let go.

Let go the peace and comfort of my cove

and dive in,

trust the current to take me

to new lands,

new adventures,

new dreams . . .

But right now

I need a few moments

to collect my thoughts,

close my eyes,

and brace myself for the cold.

Delilah

I lost my mother in September, just two weeks shy of Shaylah's first birthday. In December I lost my Boston job. This new loss actually excited me. I had been wanting to leave to start a new venture but hadn't wanted to hurt the company I was working for. They had been very, very good to me during my mother's illness. Still, this closed door meant I could tackle a new opportunity.

There was a slight problem with the new job I'd chosen: it meant relocating. Again. We had moved to Boston scarcely a year before. Doug and I decided it would be best if I took an apartment near the new job for a while, three hundred miles away, in Rochester. Doug and my eleven-year-old son would stay in Boston. My new boss was certain I'd be able to broadcast from a studio close to home within a matter of weeks, and Sonny would be able to stay in his school and on his soccer team until the season was over.

Tearfully, I packed a few bags for me and baby Shaylah and we flew to our new home away from home. The apartment was small, neat, and cozy. For months I had been incredibly busy—making funeral arrangements, cleaning out Mom's house with my sister, caring for my family, working—so I hadn't really taken time to think about the loss I had just experienced. Now, in this little apartment, with a bed, a couch, and a toddler, I had plenty of time to think and feel. There were no big meals to prepare, no piles of laundry to wash, no soccer practices to run to, nothing to distract me from the business of grief.

It is so much easier when you're busy, keeping the tears stuffed down inside. I was a bit overwhelmed by the power of the emotions I felt once I allowed myself to stop and be still. I felt all the pain that I had kept at bay with my job, my family, my responsibilities.

But slowly I began to recognize my time away in this tiny apartment as a gift. I realized that if I didn't deal with the grief I would become immobilized. I bundled Shaylah up in a soft, pink parka and headed for the beach. I held her tiny hand as we walked along the shores of Lake Ontario. I watched the seagulls soar overhead and remembered other long walks, along the beaches of our Oregon town, with my own hand tucked safely in my mother's hand. The cold wind stung my face and my tears were free to mingle with the rain.

Time passed in our little apartment. Six weeks turned into ten months. I bought ceramic paints and Shaylah picked out some little ceramic bunnies. Together we painted them and placed them in the building's flower garden.

Together we shopped for fresh fruits and vegetables in the market near the radio station. We ate frozen custard at the beach and rode the antique carousel. And gradually, my anguish turned to peace. When I first arrived at the apartment, I thought it would be a lonely, frustrating time. Instead it was a wonderful healing time, a time to bond with my little girl.

A Time to Break Down

When I was a young girl in Oregon I loved going to Girl Scout camp in the summer. I loved spending long, lazy afternoons swimming in the creek, warm nights roasting marshmallows over a fire. Mostly I loved meeting new friends and forming bonds with girls from outside my little town. I loved all aspects of camp, except when it came time to say good-bye. The counselors would yell, "OK, girls, it's time to break down," and I would. They were referring to the process of breaking down the campsite, taking the worn canvas tents down and folding them neatly away, packing up the life jackets and the paddles and the canoes. Inevitably I'd end up working through tear-filled eyes, talking in a choked voice, as I dealt with a different kind of breakdown altogether.

I have found that sometimes you have to break down before you can move on. I've spent a great deal of emotional energy trying to avoid breakdowns, trying to remain calm and in control. But sometimes it is unavoidable—and often necessary—to let down the walls of composure and go crazy, just a little. And when you stop pushing the hurt and the pain down and allow it to spill out, the healing process can begin. I've seen this process at work in my loved ones, and as hard as it is to watch without trying to prevent the pain, I know how important it can be.

Last year our adolescent daughter, Tangi, found she could no longer hold back the pain that had been stored inside her heart for most of her young life. In breaking down she was finally able to make a new beginning . . .

The mood in my car was somber. The windshield wipers beat a squeaky tune in the dark. Four-month-old Zack slept in his car seat in the back, and twelve-year-old Tangi slumped in the passenger seat by my side. She had gone to work with me to help watch the baby, and to escape the reminders of reality at home.

Tangi and her younger brother, TJ, had come to live with us six months earlier. We had been in the process of adopting their older half brother, Manny, and when we discovered that he had siblings in the foster care system, Doug and I decided to pursue custody of them as well. Then, suddenly, a crisis in their therapeutic foster home brought them to our house a lot sooner than we had anticipated. I was pregnant and on complete bed rest when they arrived. Their state caseworker dropped them off: two unhappy kids, a couple of garbage bags filled with clothes, and a ton of emotional baggage.

It was rough from the start. We had attended classes to learn how to deal with children with special needs, but we were ill prepared for three adolescents fresh from a lifetime of abuse and neglect.

We went from being a family of four to a family of eight in the blink of an eye. Where there had been relative peace, chaos now reigned. Our house was much too small to accommodate all of us, so we set about finding a bigger one. We found and purchased an old house with five bedrooms; the real estate deal closed on the same day baby Zack was born. Having more space helped to reduce some of the mayhem and confusion, but not much. Manny was adjusting well to his new home and family, but the younger two were behaving the only way they knew, after struggling for survival with drug-addicted parents, then a string of foster homes—with anger and disrespect.

Tangi's outbursts were a daily event, and try as we might, Doug and I had no clue how to cope with her mood swings and temper. TJ wasn't as volatile, but he too was prone to hysterical fits of rage, and during one of these he tore up his new bedroom. It was after one of these tantrums that the state decided we were not capable of meeting Tangi and TJ's needs. The crisis at the previous foster home had passed, and the caseworker felt they should be returned to live there. The previous caregivers were professional foster parents; they were trained to deal with dysfunctional children and had been doing so for many years. They were nice people and they cared deeply for Tangi and TJ. But they were older, had already raised their children, and weren't interested in adopting them or being a "forever family."

We knew we were in way over our heads, but we let our hearts and our faith lead us. We told the caseworkers we wanted to adopt these children, to give them the love, stability, and roots they had never known. But the state decided that our sincerity and commitment were no substitutes for an experienced foster home, and it would be best for the kids to go back there. We were disappointed and troubled, but we were also exhausted and overwhelmed. We had no choice but to give in.

So, the clock was ticking on our relationship on the night

Tangi went to work with Zacky and me. As I drove on toward home I heard her begin to sniffle, and looking over through the dark I could see tears streaming down her beautiful face. Suddenly she cried out with a scream of terror and pain. I slowed down and pulled to the side of the road. She curled up in the seat next to me and rocked her body back and forth and screamed, frightening cries of defeat and frustration. I just held her, knowing I was seeing something far beyond mere rebellion. I thought her breakdown would never end. But in a while her crying subsided, and through choked sobs, she could finally speak.

"I remember the day the police came to our apartment and took us away from our mom," she said. "Back then we were always afraid, and we never had enough food, and Mom was always gone and her boyfriend hurt us. But this hurts much worse than that. You and Dad are my family, and they can't make me leave . . . they can't make me leave. . . ." I knew at that moment I would do whatever it took to make her and her brother my own children. Up to that point Tangi had been reacting to everything with her usual attitude and rebelliousness. But all her walls tumbled down that night in my car; she declared us her family, and me her mother, and I would fight to the bitter end to keep her. The next morning Doug called the caseworkers and began the appeal process.

It's been over a year since that night, and I would love to say Tangi's temper tantrums have totally disappeared. Still, every day is a little better, as she and TJ and Manny see more evidence that we are their forever family. I'm more confident than ever that with time and counseling and prayer, my daughter and my sons will be able to overcome the pain of their past, break through the barriers that remain, and live a life filled with joy and peace.

There are days in our lives when even the smallest task can seem completely overwhelming. Work and responsibilities pile up, and the frustration of trying to be perfect can cause us to explode. But as my listener Stephanie discovered, comfort and calm can be found in the simplest places, and deep inside we know where to find them.

I remember the night well. Our family was going through a tough time financially and emotionally after the birth of our second child. We were all suffering one way or another.

This particular night, I came home from work completely exhausted. My pure-hearted six-year-old daughter, Shalene, greeted me with a bear hug as usual. I walked blindly by her—not intentionally ignoring her, but because of the hypnotic cries of my three-month-old. I carried the little one on my hip with one hand supporting his head. I knew both my children just wanted to be with Mommy, but Mommy felt overwhelmed by the demands of a new baby, another child, a home, a husband, and a stressful job.

I looked around. The house was unkempt, the children were hungry, the refrigerator was bare, and I was at my wit's end. Just then I looked out the window to see our familiar white van pull into the driveway. This sight, which usually filled me with such joy, now made me feel even more inadequate. So many women do the same things every day, and much, much more, I told myself. What makes you so special?

At that moment, the door flew open, startling me back to reality. My husband walked in and took little Thomas from my arms and kissed my cheek. He scanned the wreckage of the kitchen and said, "I guess we have a lot of work to do this weekend."

Isn't it odd how the simplest thing can set your temper ablaze? I bellowed at him, a stream-of-consciousness rant containing all my insecurities, and stomped out the still-open door. Before he could compose himself and follow, I started the car and left a streak of rubber on the driveway. I drove without cause or care for a long time, and somehow ended up in my childhood neighborhood. When I realized where I was, I knew just where I was headed—my favorite church.

It was a special place, that church. For one thing, it was kept open twenty-four hours every day. I pulled up to it and barely stopped the car before jumping out. I ran up the steps in desperation. I opened the huge, creaky door, expecting silence inside, considering the late hour. Instead, I was greeted by the most glorious hymn, sung by three beautiful voices in harmony. I slowly approached the altar, where the music was coming from, and saw the singers. I watched and listened for a while as they sang modern and ancient scores. Then one of them noticed me and asked if I would like to join them. I tried to decline, but the other two singers protested until, cornered, I gave in. I shared a score with one of them, and we took turns picking our favorite songs to sing. Despite my occasional mistakes, the music was pleasant to the ear, and more important, it was lightening my soul. We sang on until our throats were dry. When we finally called it a night, we parted with hugs. Funny, I knew no names and we exchanged only a few words, but I felt so close to them, and in such a short time. I cried on my way home that night, not out of pain or frustration but in thanksgiving.

When I got home, I kissed my husband and my two little ones as they slept in their beds. I had thought I needed to be alone. I learned that I needed to know that my contributions should not be compared to those of others. God taught me that as long as I sing from my heart, what I give is worthy.

Life can break you down, both physically and emotionally. And sometimes we lose more by trying to be strong. My listener Nicole waited a year for crucial open-heart surgery. The operation was a success, but the emotional cost of her illness was dear.

$\mathcal{L}$ooking back, it was an emotional trauma that destroyed my senior year. I had gotten to the point where nothing mattered to me anymore. I was angry, sad, confused, overwhelmed, terrified, lonely, bitter, selfish, exhausted, hollow, and numb. All I had ever wanted was for my life to be simple. I wanted the normal luxuries every other nineteen-year-old got. I wanted to worry about zits, not the consequences of a heart condition for the rest of my life. I felt like I was being punished—no one else had to deal with what I was facing. My emotions ran wild.

On the outside I seemed OK, aside from my disregard for school. I had always dealt with my problems alone—I hated dumping my life on others. I knew my friends were struggling with problems of their own. I kept so much inside it ate

away at me. I was unable to sleep or concentrate. Neverthe-
less, I worked hard to maintain my outer shell. I pretended
to be happy-go-lucky because it kept me going.

I realize my mistake now. I should have let others in. I
should have broken down and lost control. I should have
leaned on my friends and family. I made it harder for myself.
I have come to realize that despite how alone I felt, there
were so many people willing that I never opened myself up
to. I learned that my fear of appearing weak was foolish.
Struggle is something everyone endures, and if you open
your heart you never have to do it alone. Now I'm trying to
thank my friends, family, and every person I know for all
they have given me. I am forever in debt and extremely
grateful.

I've had my share of breakdowns . . . maybe more than my
share. I've learned the hard way how to let other people in,
when to give it a rest, and when to just cry it out (although that
one I didn't really have to learn!). Being human means we're
not perfect—we make mistakes, and if we let them, they can
teach us things about ourselves. I'm not proud of many things
I've done, but I sure have learned a lot. And I'm grateful for
the patience of those around me, especially my family, when I

broke down and made mistakes. I owe a special thank-you to my older brother.

Matt was—I've tried to find a more complimentary word—a geek. He was tall, thin, and gangly. For some reason his pants were always at least an inch or two too short, and his feet grew so fast he wore a size twelve man's shoe when he was in junior high, which gave him the profile of a capital *L*. If his skinny frame and lack of athletic prowess weren't enough to ensure him a slot in the nerd category, his hairstyle was. Although we grew up in the sixties and seventies, when long hair was in style, my father insisted that Matt wear a military buzz cut.

Dad wanted Matt to be a sports star, a jock. So Matt tried out for football, but he was too small to be on the line and too awkward to play any other position. He tried out for track and field, but his hay fever and asthma made running any distance an impossibility. He tried out for baseball, but he could neither throw nor hit well.

Matt loved music and playing in the pep band. He loved theater and went out for all the school productions. Mostly he loved building models of airplanes, cars, and boats. His room was filled with model planes, suspended from the ceiling with fish line.

Dad allowed us to convert a part of our attic into a work space, and it was here that my brother spent most of his free time. He had tackle boxes full of model paint—candy-apple red, jet black, and metallic gold and silver. He had shoe boxes full of small gas-powered-engine parts. He would buy sheets and blocks of balsa wood, tubes of model glue, and razor-sharp X-Acto knives. He would climb up to the attic and pull the folding stairs up behind him so the rest of us would leave him alone while he planned and cut and glued and painted and created his models.

One year, Matt decided to build a remote-controlled boat to go with his remote-controlled airplanes. He designed the plans from photographs of aircraft carriers, meticulously cutting the wood to scale. When the hull was done he cut and soaked thin strips of balsa, formed them into turret guards, and attached them to the top of the boat with Mom's sewing pins. Carefully he glued them into place. He was so proud of his handiwork. The boat was an exact replica of the photograph he had pinned on the Peg-Board above his work area.

Matt and I usually walked home from school together, and one fall day we got into an argument over something insignificant. By the time we reached our house our tempers were out of control and we were hurling insults at each other. Matt hit a particularly sensitive nerve when he called me a vulgar name and made an accusation about a boy I liked. I began to seethe.

The more I thought about it, the angrier I got. Later that

afternoon I snuck into the attic and took my rage out on Matt's new model boat. With malicious delight I lowered my thumb on the boat and systematically smashed each of the small, perfect wooden compartments he had carefully crafted and glued. I smiled as I destroyed each one, making sure to break the fragile wood into so many pieces there was no way he could restore it. When I was satisfied the destruction was complete, I quietly tiptoed downstairs and went about my evening. My anger had been satiated and I smugly, secretly delighted in my accomplishment.

Before we went to sleep that night Matt knocked on my bedroom door. With his head hung low he entered and said, "Sis, I'm really sorry for those things I said. I don't know why I called you that name. You're a great sister and I apologize." My heart sank to my feet. Here stood the object of my rage, sincerely apologizing for the argument that had driven me to my destructive act. I was stunned. I swallowed hard and said, "That's OK." I couldn't sleep that night. I tossed and turned and tried to figure out how to tell him what I had done.

The next afternoon Matt went directly to the stuffy attic, and in only a moment I heard his anguished scream as he discovered his precious boat, totally destroyed. He flew down the stairs two at a time and burst into the back room, panting, his eyes wild. "Where's Timmy?" he bellowed, assuming our baby brother had been the one who climbed the stairs and ruined his project.

I stood there, speechless and horrified. In my humiliation and shame I wanted to confess to the crime and ask his forgiveness. And then I looked at the anger on his face, and I swallowed hard and said, "I don't know, but if I see him I'll catch him and hold him so you can beat his butt."

I'd like to be able to tell you that I bravely owned up to what I did, but I didn't. I would prefer to say this was a thoughtless and impulsive act, but I considered everything carefully and decided I didn't wish to feel Matt's wrath. I don't remember whether I actually helped him catch Timmy, but I can't swear I didn't. My memory, usually so reliable, fails me on this one.

I would love to say that I had an opportunity to get honest with Matthew and tell him the truth about the smashed boat while he was alive. I didn't. I would love to say that I never did another mean, rotten, spiteful thing in anger. I can't. But looking back, this was the first time I knew in my heart that my anger was destructive and hurtful, and I felt the pain of my actions deeper than I wanted to.

I'd like to think that I learned something about myself that afternoon in the attic, and something about how I'd like to be from my brother that evening. I learned that I was human and imperfect, capable of hurting the ones I loved. But I also learned the power of forgiveness. I didn't recognize it then, and I certainly didn't change overnight. But Matt taught me something that day that I'll always treasure. He showed me that anger is weak but there is strength in admitting when we've done wrong, and in forgiveness.

I hope my little brother, Tim, has forgiven me for not learning that lesson sooner!

A Time to Build Up

Our family lived on the Oregon coast, just a few minutes from the ocean. My father's parents, Grandma and Grandpa Luke, had a house that was only a few feet from the bay. Both of my grandfathers were avid fishermen, and my grandmothers were equally skilled at digging clams and catching crabs. So, we children spent many long, wonderful hours at the beach.

The beaches of Oregon are a bit different from those I've visited on the East Coast or in southern California. They're much cooler, even in the middle of summer, and the wind is usually brisk. We lived in the heart of the Oregon Dunes, a national recreation area that stretches for many miles. The white sand dunes rolled on as far as your eyes could see, and the beaches were usually empty, except for piles of driftwood and an occasional neighbor or friend digging clams or walking a dog.

Mom would pile us in the back of the old station wagon—my brothers and sister and a neighbor friend or two. We would take our plastic shovels and pails along, and off we would go to play in the sand. Our mother loved the beach as much as we did. She would walk with us close to the water's edge and help us find perfect sand dollars, broken clamshells, twisted driftwood, and small pieces of polished beach glass. We would fill our buckets with the sea's offerings. Sometimes we'd take our buckets of goodies home, but mostly we used them as construction materials for elaborate sand castles.

We'd pick a spot not too far from the water's edge because we wanted the sand to be damp enough to hold together. Yet it had to be far enough up the beach that the waves wouldn't come crashing down and destroy our masterpiece.

We worked for hours building towers and turrets, and we always finished the castle off with a drawbridge and a moat. If we planned it right and timed it correctly, the moat would fill with seawater as we dug down to the level of the ocean. If our timing was off we'd have either an empty moat or a crumbling castle.

The bucket of treasures collected at the water's edge was incorporated into our design. A clamshell might become a window, a piece of driftwood served as a flagstaff, a piece of seaweed as the flag. My brother Matt would plan and design and bark orders. My little sister, DeAnna, would usually be the one he barked at. Her job was to bring more sand, making sure it wasn't too wet, and to find more shells and sticks. I got to decorate the towers with polished stones and bits of glass, and then I would carve pictures into the sides of our fortress. Timmy usually tried to kick it down with his chubby little legs.

For hours we worked and played and laughed and argued as a family. And then the tide would turn and the waves would sneak up on us. Frantically we would try to build walls to protect our castle, laughing as we raced against time. But the ocean always won, and our castles were soon eaten by the hungry waves, disappearing into the dark waters in far less time than it took us to build them.

But though the castles always dissolved, our family ties solidified. We four children learned to cooperate and communicate, and we learned how to work together to build something as a team. I don't know if my mother was aware that her gift of time at the ocean's edge was more than a time of laughter and fun. It was a time that helped build bonds that have lasted my entire life and memories that will warm me in my old age.

I once heard a wise man speak on the importance of relationships. He stressed that anytime we embark upon a project or set out to plan an event, we should remember that the project and the event aren't what matters—it's the relationships we establish and strengthen during the project that mean the most.

Every person born has different talents, different skills, different insights. If these gifts are encouraged, nurtured, and built up, they'll develop into skills that can bless a multitude of people. My mom had her faults, but one of her strong points was as a cheerleader for her children, an encourager. She made me feel that nothing was impossible. She made me see that what Mr. Thoreau said is true: "If you have built castles in the air, your work need not be lost; that is where they should be. Now put the foundations under them."

My older brother has since gone on to live in another kind of castle. While my little sister no longer meekly follows those who bark orders at her, she is still resourceful and responsible. Timmy, the baby, is busy helping his children learn to build sculptures in the Oregon sand, and I am still a dreamer, building castles in the air.

When you reach out in love and build someone up, you usually end up building yourself up as well. Whether it is something as fleeting as a warm smile, or holding a door open for an elderly person, or sacrificing your seat on a crowded subway so a tired mother can sit with her child, a small act of kindness goes a long way.

My listener Patti experienced this when she was in college and spent her Saturday mornings teaching crafts to a group of twelve-year-old developmentally disabled girls. One mother told Patti and her fellow teachers that her daughter had fallen behind the other girls in school because she couldn't tie her shoes. Patti writes:

*M*y teaching partner spent time with the girl the first week but made no progress. I was next. All the following Friday night I worried about how I was going to teach her to tie her shoes. What was the key? Then I remembered I had noticed that she was a leftie. Well, I'm a rightie, and I can hardly do anything with my left hand—so how must it be for a left-handed person? I jumped out of bed at two in the morning, grabbed my tennis shoe, and tried to teach myself to tie my shoes backward. At first it was a fiasco, but finally I mastered it.

Next morning I got up early and practiced. When my turn to teach the girl came, I sat her in my lap and started, slowly, to make a loose knot, then a loop, and then I pulled the shoestring through and completed the knot. "Now, you try it," I said. The first time she fumbled a bit . . . but the second time, she did it. She screamed for joy—so loud she scared the other girls. Then she threw her arms around my neck and hugged me. I said, "Now let's practice," and she did it time and again.

When her mom arrived later that Saturday, the girl was the first out the door, screaming, "Mom, I did it." Her mother looked at me in astonishment. She told me everyone had tried to teach her—she, her husband, the teacher—all to no avail. When I told her how I'd done it, I had to teach her, too. Practice makes perfect. And the next Saturday, when the girl arrived, she was wearing shoes she had tied all by herself.

If you're wise, you'll pay attention to the people who influence you, and appreciate what they give you. People pass through our lives and leave their marks on us . . . teachers, friends, bosses, neighbors. Whether or not they stay near us, they stay in our hearts always. I asked one of my best childhood friends, Dee Dee—who, thank God, is still in my life—to write about someone special to her.

When Aunty Zoe was born, horses were still the main form of transportation. The first time I saw her she was enduring the noise of a jumbo jet landing, leaning over the fence of my mother-in-law-to-be's in-the-flight-path backyard, pained smile on her face, ever-present cigarette between her fingers.

I was twenty years old and new to Seattle's big-city attitude. Aunty Zoe was a young and feisty seventy. I lived with her for the last few months before Steve and I got married, sharing her cozy little house next door.

Back in Oregon I remember telling Delilah I was moving to Seattle and getting married. She was teasing her big eighties hairdo at the time, and said, "Ha! Right!" When I borrowed my hair curlers back for the move north, she believed me (I think she was mostly crying over the loss of the curlers).

Life in Seattle was daunting to a small-town girl like me. But though she was a stranger—just my new family's next-door neighbor—Aunty Zoe and I connected from the first day, and she quickly became my guide, teacher, and confidante. She was born to be an aunt.

"Today we're going downtown for a little ratty shopping," she said, which meant she was going to introduce me to the wonders of what she claimed was the biggest Goodwill store in the country. I didn't dare doubt it. We came home loaded with treasures. But not without a long lunch, the first of many, at her favorite funky diner. I came home loaded with cholesterol, too.

And on the way, she insisted I drive, gripping the steering wheel, grimly determined to survive. I'm from a town with two stoplights. Zoe smoked and chatted away, marveling at the changes in the city since her arrival and describing other, more inept drivers in language more appropriate to the Seattle waterfront of 1932. It was a whole new phase of my education.

I got so much from Aunty Zoe, even a taste for strong black coffee in the morning. I never got the hang of those cigarettes, fortunately, but there was plenty more education that I've used every day since. It was only a few months, but I think I grew up in Aunty Zoe's house. She was tough and gentle, wise to life's absurdities but full of faith and strength. She is still my inspiration to take life as it comes.

Dee Dee

Even though I am in the communication field, I often forget about the power of the spoken word. Our words have the power to hurt or to heal, and a kind word can change your whole perspective. Jennie wrote me about how a stranger took a risk and gave her a wonderful gift.

I'd had an incredibly stressful week. My senior project was due, my friend was having problems with an eating disorder, and my ex-boyfriend was doing his best to tear me down.

Instead of working on my project, I found myself at a twenty-fifth-anniversary celebration for a dear couple I know from church. As I was standing in the food line, a voice next to me said, "Hey, beautiful." I looked up. It was an older man. I smiled and went about my business. He said, "Do you know you're beautiful?"

At this point I thought, This guy has got to have problems—he's old enough to be my grandpa, and here he is hitting on me. I mumbled something about not ever really thinking about it.

He replied, "Well, we both know that you just lied to me, God, and your parents, now, don't we?" Now I was curious about what would come next. He said, "God don't make no junk. All his creations are beautiful. Therefore, you are beautiful."

My face must have turned red as a tomato. It's strange how rarely we are told we're beautiful—and how important it is for us, especially us teenagers, to hear it. I decided maybe this man didn't have a problem after all.

A few days later I replayed the whole thing, taking the older gentleman's role, for my friend with the weight worries. I asked her if she knew she was beautiful. I insisted she say it. In a little while she was smiling. By the end of the evening, we were both amazed at how her outlook had changed—not to mention mine.

Thanks to a stranger, Jennie's confidence got a boost . . . and she learned a new skill—how to help another person to accept herself as a unique and beautiful creation. And then she passed it on. I learned a similar lesson recently—a wake-up call from a simple but inspiring man that made me appreciate the wonderful life I've been given. Now I pass that reminder on to you.

I had to go away for a short business trip one weekend, and since Doug was busy, I took a taxi to the airport. The driver was an older gentleman, impeccably dressed in slacks and a sport jacket. He met me at the front door of our house and cheerfully took my overnight bag. He introduced himself as George, and led me to his taxi. I was amazed when I saw it. The paint shone with many layers of wax and the interior appeared to be brand new. The camel-colored seats were covered with clear plastic to keep them spotless. "I've never seen such a lovely cab," I said.

"It's because I don't lease it, I own it," George replied in a heavy accent. "I take care of the things I love. Of course, I do not love this car, not like I love my wife and my children." He told me he and his wife had been married over forty-eight years, and she was still "so beautiful."

As he drove on, he talked about his life. He had been a child in Warsaw when his people took a stand against Hitler. He told me of losing his entire family in the Ghetto Uprising, of being shot in the side but still carrying on, of his fourteen months in a concentration camp. Throughout his story, he always returned to his wife, his children, and his grandchildren.

"People here have no idea how wonderful their lives are," he said. "Because I lived through hell, I appreciate all that I have today."

Most of us haven't seen the agony of war and destruction, so it's understandable that we take our lives for granted. This man, who is clearly the best, proudest taxi owner-driver in town, has made it his mission to be a builder as well—to make sure everyone he comes in contact with realizes how much we have. It was just a taxi ride to the airport, but this man turned it into a significant excursion. I spent the rest of my trip counting my blessings.

When I received this letter from Lori-Ann I had just given birth to my baby Zacky, and I was feeling overwhelmed with all my responsibilities. When I read her letter, and the amazing sacrificial gift her parents gave her and her new infant, I cried tears of joy for her. My children have grown up so quickly, and I know the minutes and hours that I am able to spend with them will help to determine who they become in the future. I want to give my children a million wonderful gifts, but mostly I want to give them the gift of my uninterrupted, undivided attention. In order to do that I have to have the time to spend with them. Lori-Ann's mother and father understood how quickly children grow, and gave their daughter an amazing gift of time.

*A*lthough they say you can't buy time, my parents gave me the greatest gift of all by doing just that. When my first child, Alex, was born, I knew that I'd have to return to work as soon as my maternity leave was up—we couldn't afford to give up my salary. I interviewed baby-sitters and toured day care centers, but nothing seemed quite right. I couldn't imagine leaving my son for the entire day with complete strangers—because of the length of my commute, his caregivers would actually be spending more time with my son than I would.

Then one day, just a few weeks before I was due to go back to work, my mother handed me a greeting card envelope addressed to my son. Inside was an extremely generous check, and a handwritten card: "Alex: The bottom line is . . . having Mom at home is the best, and we want only the very best for you. With all our love, Grandma and Grandpa." My parents aren't rich . . . they're both public school teachers. Because of their generosity, I was able to quit my job and stay home with my son. They told me to think of it as an early inheritance.

Now, when I see Alex reach each new milestone—his

first smile, turning over on his own, grasping his first rattle—my heart swells with love for him, and for my parents, who kept me from missing these "firsts." They gave me the gift of time, and I couldn't be more thankful.

When we think of building someone up, we often imagine major, life-changing acts, like what Lori-Ann's parents did. But you don't have to pay all of someone's expenses, or help a person find a job, or teach a child to read to make something beautiful happen. Every day we're given small opportunities to bring someone joy that can make a huge difference in a life. My husband, Doug, got a chance to give one little boy a great experience, and despite some unexpected bumps in the road, he was able to deliver even more than he expected to—with a little divine help. I asked him to write his story down.

Skip was just eleven years old. He'd come from a divorced family and had experienced traumatic hardships as he moved around the country with one parent and two siblings. He was angry with his parents and with his life. When I met him, he was tall and lanky and, surprisingly, carried a big youthful smile on his face. It was obvious to me that despite his troubled life, his innocence hadn't been totally destroyed. We became friends.

One day I heard that a Christian rock group I liked was performing in Boston and I thought, Wouldn't this be a great experience for Skip? I wanted him to have some fun and some good memories while he was still a kid. Without hesitation, his mother gave us permission to go.

My best friend, Billy, had planned to take our church youth group to the concert. I asked him if he could purchase two extra tickets for Skip and me. He said there'd be no problem.

There was no way Billy could have known that the church parents' committee would decide only kids over twelve would be allowed to go to the concert. No way for him to predict that even after talking to the church committee, I wouldn't be able to get a pair of tickets. And that just a couple of hours before show time, an eager young boy would be waiting for me to take him to a concert for which I had no way in.

What was I going to do? I had no idea. But without a single solution in my head I left my house, got into my truck, and drove off to pick Skip up. I prayed all the way there . . . I said, "God, you know my heart. This is for Skip, not for me. If there's anything you could do, please help me."

When Skip got into the truck, I explained to him that I had a little problem getting the tickets earlier and that I'd stop by to see what they had left. I told him not to worry. Skip just smiled and smiled. I was on some kind of autopilot and prayed all the way to the ticket office.

In an uncomfortably short time we arrived, and I told Skip to wait for me in the truck. If there were no tickets, I wanted the bad news to come from me and not from a stranger behind a counter. I walked in and asked if there were any tickets available to the concert. "For tonight?" said the clerk.

"Yes," I said, red faced. "Tonight."

"OK, I'll check, but I don't know if we'll find anything this close to show time." Her fingers rattled the keyboard. I stared at her face, lit by the glow of the computer screen. Within seconds, she said, "OK, I found some seats, but I don't know if you'll like them." I didn't care where they were. I just wanted to get in the door. I said I'd take them. Then, as her fingers clickety-clicked, her eyebrows rose. "What is it?" I said.

"Well . . ." She paused for a moment. "I don't believe it. But there they are."

"What?" I almost shouted.

"They weren't there before, but they're there now."

"What's there?!"

"Let me show you." She drew a rectangular shape in the air with her fingers. "Here's the stage"—and pointing directly to what would be front and center, she said, "and here's you."

After paying, I ran to the truck, gripping the precious tickets. Skip was waiting with a huge smile on his face and was practically bouncing in his seat as I approached.

When we arrived at the front door of the Orpheum, I could feel the electricity in the air. I handed the tickets to an usher and heard the words, "Oh! Right this way, sir." Moses could not have parted the

Red Sea any better than these ushers parting the crowd. Level by level, the crowd opened up to reveal closer and closer seating. We arrived at our destination, grabbed our seats, and sat down. I looked over at Skip. All the money in the world could not have replaced seeing his beautiful, bright young smile. Skip felt special. An awesome sense of joy overtook me. I quietly lifted my eyes and said, "Thank you, Lord." While we waited for the opening band, I glanced around the auditorium to see if I could spot the youth group from my church. I found them. From far up in the nosebleed section, Billy acknowledged that he saw me too, with a wave and a shaken fist. I laughed. I laughed really loud.

I have known lots of teachers, watched as they worked long hours for little reward. Teachers help to shape our future because they shape our children's lives. Because of their efforts and energies they are often building up the lives of others; it's their job. When Dave was a twenty-one-year-old student teacher in Pennsylvania, he learned how powerful his position as a teacher could be, and how great his responsibility to honor his role.

*A*s part of our college course work during the six weeks we spent student teaching, we had to work one-on-one with a student and keep a journal. I selected the brightest, cutest kid in the room because I thought he would be easy to work with. My college professor, however, had another idea. He insisted I work with a student I had been having problems with the first few days.

Stewart was a very small boy, almost sickly. He never smiled, and he was clearly way behind in all subjects. So I began spending the hour-a-day time with him working on projects and helping him with his studies. I recorded all the work in my journal each night.

At first Stewart tried my patience; he was so slow compared to the other kids. I really doubted that I was getting through to him. As the days and weeks passed I began to learn more about Stewart, more than a young student teacher was ready to learn. Stewart had been abused by family members and was often left alone in the house. He came to school in part to get away from the sadness in his home.

By the end of the six weeks we got along OK. Stewart's slowness was still hard to deal with, but I thought I had helped him out. Then, on the last day I was there, the class's teacher had each child make a farewell card for me. I looked over them. Most of the cards were covered with lovely drawings and sweet sayings.

Then I came to a plain white card with the words "To Mr. Weaver" scrawled on the front. I knew this was Stewart's—he never colored anything. I opened the card. Written inside, in that same distinctive scrawl, was, "I wish you were my dad."

I felt overwhelmed and ashamed. I had given this young boy a small piece of my attention for a short time and he had so cherished it. I never again questioned whether I could have an impact on children as a teacher in ways that really matter—feeling loved, feeling self-respect. Stewart taught me that.

I left the teaching profession years ago, but that white card, that little boy, and his lesson have been in the background of my life for all these years. Stewart, I hope you are well, and well loved.

When we asked our adoption caseworker to look into the possibility of getting custody of our adopted son Manny's two siblings, who were still in foster care, she looked at my husband and me as if we had gone off the deep end.

She explained the high level of problems with both children, especially the younger of the two, TJ. He was nine years old at the time, and like his siblings, he had bounced around most of his young life. For some reason he was more aggressive than the others, she explained, and she didn't think he would be able to calm down and fit into a regular family. At the time he was in a therapeutic foster home, and even highly trained caregivers were having a difficult time handling his outbursts. He had kicked down a door at a previous preadoptive placement, completely destroyed his principal's office, and been kicked out of school so many times the caseworker had lost count. He had thrown a baseball through a window, smashed up his bedroom, beat his angry fists against walls. She had known the kids since they were taken from their biological family, and she assured us that TJ was incorrigible.

"He seems to get some sort of high from being hurtful and angry," she explained. Could this be the same boy we had taken camping for a week just a month before? The same sweet child who had held my hand in the dark as we sat around the campfire and sang songs, the same young boy who timidly asked if he could call me Mom since he didn't have a real mom anymore?

Doug and I didn't want to make a decision that would harm our young daughter or the baby we were expecting, but we just didn't see the monster that the caseworker described. Doug and I felt that God wanted us to bring the other two children into our family, so we assured Iona, the caseworker, that we wanted to start out slowly, with visitations on weekends for several months. After our baby was born and we had a chance to settle in with our infant, we could discuss bringing the other two children into our home. For one thing, we knew we would need to start looking for a bigger house.

Iona shook her head and again told us how destructive TJ's anger was and how she didn't think it would work, especially with two young children in the house. The way she talked he sounded like a child who belonged in an institution, and indeed he had been hospitalized twice in his young life for his destructive outbursts and had been given medication to modify his behavior.

Doug and I prayed and continued to have weekly visitations with the children. We had gone from a family of two to a family of three with Manny's adoption, and now we were expecting a baby and talking about taking on two more children. Maybe Iona was right, maybe we were way out of our league. And yet I kept seeing TJ's sweet face as he looked up at me and said, "I don't have a real mom anymore."

When I was six months pregnant we got the kids for Christmas vacation, and then because of bad weather we had them for an extra four days. We were stressed, but my heart broke when they had to return to their foster home.

In February they came for winter break, and during that time there was a tragedy in their foster family, so they stayed. And they stayed. In my seventh month there were complications with my pregnancy and I was placed on bed rest.

During one week in March our two older boys were away with their school on a mission trip. Tangi was staying with some old friends from a previous foster placement, leaving TJ and Shaylah the only two at home. It was spring break so I assumed TJ would want to sleep in and have a nice, leisurely day without the older kids harassing him. The first morning the others were gone I woke to the smell of sausage frying. TJ appeared at my bedroom door with a tray in his hand. "Good morning, Mom," he half whispered, and presented the tray.

Rubbing the sleep out of my eyes I tried to raise up on one elbow, not an easy task with my pregnant belly. There on the tray were two eggs, cooked the way I like them, with the yolks runny, two pieces of buttered toast, and two sausage patties. "Did Dad cook breakfast?" I asked.

"No, Mom, I wanted to surprise you so I got up early and cooked breakfast for you." When I was finished eating he took the tray back to the little kitchen and appeared once again at my bedroom door. He asked if he could come in, and I scooted over in bed so he could sit next to me. He took my hand and just sat there, asking me simple questions about the baby—what names we had decided on, where we were going to put the crib, what hospital I would be going to. Looking at his handsome young face, I knew the baby in my belly was going to have another wonderful older brother to love.

Since he has been a part of our family TJ has had only one

angry outburst. There have been no kicked-in doors, no broken windows, no fists smashed against walls. I have to wonder if the many prescriptions for mood-altering medications he had been given in the past were written in place of the thing he most needed, a forever family to love him. TJ has now settled in as if he had been born to us. And at least once a week my thoughtful son brings me breakfast in bed.

A Time to Weep

I'm a sap. I can't help it. I seem to be tear-duct challenged. I cry. I cry through *Hallmark Hall of Fame* movies. I cry every time I watch *Fried Green Tomatoes*. I *really* cry when I watch *Beaches*. I even cry at "Reach out and touch someone" AT&T commercials.

I cry when people get married. I cry even harder when people get divorced. I cry when babies are born and I cry out of control when they die.

I cry when I'm PMSing. I cry when I'm not.

I cry when my children get hurt. I cry when my feelings get hurt. I cry when I watch the news and someone I don't even know gets hurt. I cry when an ambulance goes screaming by, lights flashing.

I cry when I look at photos of the family members I have lost to death. I cry when I look at photos of my children and see how fast they've grown. I cry when a listener calls whose heart has been shattered. I cry even harder for them off the air. I cry when I'm miserable, and I cry when I'm ecstatic. Sometimes I laugh until I cry.

I get asked to do a lot of public speaking. Even though I'm grateful for the opportunity to share insights with a large audience, I'm always embarrassed when I speak on a subject that is close to my heart, because I know halfway through my speech I'm going to lose it and cry. It's frustrating to have words in my heart that I want to speak, then to feel them catch in my throat when it closes down and tears spring to my eyes—whether I'm speaking on behalf of the Children's Miracle Network or about the joys and frustrations of special-needs adoption. Whether I am preaching or teaching or just talking to a group of women for a Mother's Day luncheon, it seems I always end up crying.

I watch actresses on TV and I wonder how they do it: silver globes of sadness slip down their serene faces, they look pitiful and radiant and beautiful all at the same time. Not me. My nose swells up and turns brilliant red like Rudolph in the old Christmas classic, and I take on a nasal tone. I have to sniff and snort to clear my sinuses, my eyes puff up and nearly swell shut. My tears streak my makeup, my neck gets bright scarlet splotches, and I look like I have hives. Not a pretty sight. One day I hope to gain the composure, the grace, the dignity to stop crying so much, or at least figure out how to look good while I'm doing it . . .

But then, maybe it doesn't matter. I remember the story I heard about a little girl and her best friend walking home from school. The friend was carrying her precious porcelain doll—she'd taken it to school for show-and-tell—and she suddenly dropped it to the sidewalk, and it shattered. The little girl helped her friend pick up the pieces, and this took quite a bit of time—there were so many pieces. She got home late, and her mother met her at the door. "What kept you so long?" she demanded. "I was worried about you." The girl explained about her friend's broken doll. Her mother admonished her, "You didn't have to wait. There was nothing you could do that would fix that doll."

"I know, Mom," the little girl said. "I stayed to help her cry."

For a healthy person, crying is you at your most honest. The emotion, whether sorrow or joy, takes over your body and for that time you *are* the emotion and the emotion is you. It can overtake you when you're alone, hiding in the shower. Or the dam may burst when you're sharing joy or sorrow with the people you love. For a little while, you are out of control, in the best way.

And then it stops, and you know that the tide has crested, and while it may only be for a while—there may be more to come—you feel release and relief. And amazingly, you feel stronger than before. Crying a sign of weakness? No way. It is the strongest among us who can weep. Weakness is stiff and brittle, and it breaks. Strength bends. Weeping is, maybe, the most important ability God has given us. It's hard to be cruel when you're crying.

Some Christmas season, I hope I'll be able to sit and watch *It's a Wonderful Life* without tears streaming down my ruddy face. Maybe, in a few years, I'll make it through my son's graduation without bawling like a fool as he walks up to get his diploma. But probably not. More likely I will let go, and embrace the emotion, and feel it as intensely as I can. I can only hope that by then I will have found a way to cry and look terrific at the same time. Or maybe I'll have finally learned . . . to weep is beautiful.

Tears are important, and so often they're the only thing we can say about a situation . . . and the most eloquent. It was two nights before Elizabeth's best friend was to leave for the air force, and the gang from school had gathered for dinner. Elizabeth writes:

$\mathscr{J}$t was nothing fancy, just the gang hanging around the table, talking, watching a movie, and eating. No pictures were taken and no sad speeches during the dinner. It was just lots of talk and laughter.

Then everyone was leaving, and we all walked out on my porch to say good-bye. That's when the tears started. It was starting to rain, and so were we, and we all stood hanging on to one another. We all knew that even when my friend came back on leave, it wouldn't be the same. We were all leaving—going to college, growing up, moving in different directions. For those few moments on the porch, time stood still for the last time, as we cried together and said good-bye.

Even if your job demands that you grow a tough hide, tears aren't a sign of weakness—they can actually make you stronger. People in the helping professions know that they don't do the people they're trying to help any favors by trying to be detached. And even where toughness is absolutely necessary, there is a place for compassion and empathy.

Laura is a listener who works as a private security guard. Her ambition is to become a police officer; her job is to look for trouble. One night she found a person in trouble and discovered the strength that comes from taking the time to care.

I was patrolling a back alley at night when I saw a person lying under a ratty old blanket on an old couch someone had left out for the garbage truck. As I approached, I was a little on edge, expecting to be cussed at, preparing myself for a confrontation. I called, "Hey are you OK?" I wanted to make sure I was approaching a living person and not a dead body. From under the blanket I heard, "Yes ma'am!" The blanket was pulled back and an older black gentleman looked out at me. I said, "You know you can't loiter in the alley."

He said, "Oh, I'll be on my way. I just wanted to rest my knee. I got beat up by some gang boys, and I needed to rest because I also got a gunshot wound in my back." I was shocked, and I asked him if he needed medical attention. He said he was treated and released from the hospital the day before.

I felt pain like a knife through my heart at how cold I sounded, trying to be tough. But I couldn't be and I didn't want to be. I looked at him for a moment, then I said, "Don't worry, sir, just go ahead and rest yourself for the night."

All night this man weighed on my mind and brought tears to my eyes. I made hourly checks on him but didn't disturb his sleep. My shift ended at five in the morning. I was drained, but before I went home I stopped by a neighborhood store and bought an apple, a sandwich, and some hot chocolate and took them back to the old man on the couch in the alley. He thanked me and tried to sit up, but shook so bad in pain that I told him to stay put.

The next night I sobbed and prayed he would still be in that alley. Much to my relief, he was still there when I came through. I woke him up and asked him if he was able to get up and move around. He said he could and thanked me for letting him rest. He sounded much better. I asked him his name. "Scotty," he said.

I said, "Scotty, my name is Laura. I'll be through every hour tonight, so please let me know if you need *anything.*"

He said, "Oh, love, thank you very much, Laura. You're an angel. Yes ma'am, I'll let you know."

As I think about Scotty I start to cry. I have spent so much time in my job trying to become a cop—busting people, which I could easily have done to Scotty. God reminded me that I wanted to be a cop to help people, to touch a life or two. Even though I will probably never see him again, I'll always keep Scotty with me.

His tender, full lower lip quivered and angry tears filled his beautiful eyes. "I can't rake the leaves!" he moaned, and threw himself on the mound in the middle of the yard.

Sonny was ten. I had just given birth to his younger sister, Shaylah. My husband was out of town and I was newly unemployed. We lived in a nice house with a huge maple tree in the small front yard—a huge maple tree filled with brightly colored maple leaves. Leaves that were now falling and covering every inch of our property. It was a lovely neighborhood of much more expensive homes than ours, with their manicured, leaf-free lawns and neat window boxes. I was cranky, exhausted, and tired of looking out my streaked windows at piles of rotting leaves. So I had bundled my son up and sent him out to work.

Several times he came back in the house, complaining that the leaves were too wet, they were too heavy, his arms ached, he was bored, and he simply couldn't finish the task. I snapped, "Stop complaining and get back to your rake."

Now, standing at the front door, I saw his frustrated face and tears of anguish, and I knew that he was overwhelmed by the task I'd given him. I recognized what he was going through—the feeling of being totally incapable of handling the situation. Hadn't I felt the same way myself lately? So I called Sonny inside, fixed him a cup of hot cocoa, and sent him upstairs to his room to rest.

Since that day I've found myself in any number of situations where I simply couldn't deal with the daunting task before me—times when I've felt so exhausted and overwhelmed that I simply couldn't take another step. Now, when frustration takes over my heart and threatens to steal my joy, I lift my eyes to the heavens, and cry out, "God, I can't rake the leaves!" and I know He understands. And then I stop a moment and let myself rest.

A Time to Laugh

From my father I inherited my blue eyes, my flat butt, and my offbeat sense of humor. From my mother's side of the family I got my high cheekbones, my knock-knees, and my loud laugh. My really loud laugh.

Years ago I dated a man named Bob a few times. He wouldn't take me to see funny movies because he said I laughed too loud and embarrassed him. Notice, I said I dated him "a few times." They got fewer after that comment. I would do a lot of things to cement a relationship in those days, but give up laughing? No way. There must always be time for laughter, for the sake of your soul, and a funny movie is definitely one way to find it.

The ability to laugh is an important test when considering a relationship. My producer, Jane, has a friend named Anne. Anne is bright, young, pretty, ambitious, and single. She wants to be married. She wants to have children and a house in the suburbs. She was dating a handsome man named Mike for some time and things seemed to be heading down that well-known path toward monogrammed napkins and homely bridesmaids' dresses. Mike had a good job, loved to hike and ski, and even knew how to cook. And then, out of the blue, Anne decided to dump him. When Jane asked her friend why things ended so abruptly, she replied, "He just wasn't funny." Others would probably think she was crazy, but Jane and I understood completely.

When I met my husband, Doug, he was very young. Very, very young. He was twenty-three, living at home with his folks. He owned a bicycle and a fish tank. He had injured his back working on the lobster docks and his car engine had blown up, so he was recuperating from his injury and hanging out with his friends.

I was thirty-two, had a busy career and a young son. Not a lot of common ground there. But during our first real conversation he made me laugh. He made me laugh a lot. He stole my heart with his quick wit and his irresistible laugh. People who can laugh—and make others laugh and feel good—are loving people, the sort of people I want to spend my life with. OK . . . the fact that he was adorable didn't hurt.

I have a wonderful circle of friends who all have the gift of laughter, the gift of humor. Many of them could be stand-up comedians if they weren't busy raising children or running accounting firms or producing my radio show. The two people who help create my show each night, Peter and Jane, can make jokes out of just about any situation. If our listeners heard the humor that goes on behind the microphone they would no doubt be shocked. Jane and Peter once produced a rap song from a phone call where a listener told me about his twenty-two-year-old, toothless, hairless dog, Uggie. The listener was quite serious when he told us how his dog climbed into his dead wife's coffin. Somehow, the image of a dog with a bald rear end jumping into a coffin spoiled the seriousness of his story for us. I hope that listener doesn't mind that he and Uggie gave us a much-needed, loving laugh.

My friend Dee Dee and I have been close since we were children. We get together often, and within minutes I'm laughing so hard my children think I have lost my mind. We laugh about the silly things that happen in our daily lives—the way her dog follows her into the bathroom, and when she slams the door in his face he tries to push his nose under it. So she sprays air freshener at the floor to make him sneeze.

The way her brainiac son could virtually disassemble a Learjet when he was five, and her husband, the actual Learjet pilot, can't assemble a TV tray. We laugh about our ex-boyfriends, and our days in disco dresses and halter tops. We laugh about our sagging boobs and hemorrhoids, our bottled hair color and big feet. The fact that we can laugh about ourselves together puts even the most embarrassing things into perspective.

We need laughter, even on the most solemn occasions. Before my mom passed away she requested that we not have a funeral, but hold a celebration of her life. So at the memorial service we asked her family members and friends to stand and share their favorite Wilma stories. The entire church rang with laughter as one person after another shared these delightful, silly stories of my mother and her antics.

For instance, there was Wilma's Magic Elixir: when we were sick, my mother would make an amazing drink that she guaranteed would make us well. It was a combination of carrot juice, egg whites, and soda pop. Mom was so insistent that this was a miracle cure, she had all her friends mixing it up and giving it to their kids whenever they came down with anything. It became a local legend—carrot juice, egg whites, soda pop— and the kids got well. Looking back, we couldn't say whether it was the life-giving properties of Mom's concoction or the idea of being forced to drink more of the bizarre stuff that miraculously restored the children of our town to health.

I have heard it said that angels can fly because they take

themselves lightly. I'm glad I was blessed with my dad's bent sense of humor and my mother's loud laugh. They help me keep my feet just far enough off the ground to feel like I might take flight.

Laughter is at its best when it takes you by surprise. But you can always count on children to supply comedy, especially when they're not trying to be funny but are attempting to explain the world around them. I love this story Melissa sent me about her five-year-old's view of modern technology:

*O*ne day, while we were driving somewhere, my daughter said, "I know how cars work . . . God's son, Jesus, has a remote control and he makes everyone's car go straight." I said, "That's a cute idea, honey, but if Jesus is controlling the cars with a remote, how come people get into automobile accidents?" She answered immediately, "That's when God tells Jesus, 'Come here!' And he leaves the remote on the couch and doesn't watch it."

I try to do things with and for my kids that will make lasting memories. I try to stimulate their creativity and encourage them to express themselves.

One weekend I planned a little arts and crafts project. I went to the hardware store and bought a bag of cement, then picked up some forms for stepping-stones from the local arts and crafts store. Then I rushed about from one secondhand shop to another, searching for dishes that had been chipped or cracked, colorful pieces of pottery that would make a lovely mosaic. I came home with two bags of plates, saucers, and cups.

I separated the china into color schemes: blues with blues, greens with greens. Then I placed the pieces in double paper bags and gave them to Sonny, Manny, and little Shaylah, and sent them out to the patio to break the dishes into small pieces, so we could use the fragments to decorate stepping-stones.

I thought they would delight in placing the colorful pieces in patterns, creating wonderful works of art with their tender hands. I envisioned lovely stepping-stones, created by each of the kids as a lasting reminder of our fun together. I pictured the four of us working closely as a group on the basement floor, bonding as a family . . . And then I discovered the greatest fun they would get out of the project was dropping the double bags of plates on the cement patio!

They laughed, they squealed, delighted to be breaking the plates! They came back into the house again and again, begging for more pieces to break. I asked the boys why it was so much fun. Sonny said, "All my life you're telling me to be careful, don't play ball in the house, don't break the good glasses, and now you're letting me break this china. This is great, Mom!"

The stepping-stones turned out great, too, and we did have a wonderful time together as we made lovely designs. But the kids would have settled for the joy of breaking a few ten-cent plates, laughing the whole time.

As you might expect, a person like me, who likes to laugh, is attracted to people who create laughter. But my particular circle of friends isn't satisfied tossing off one-liners or sending crazy greeting cards. No, they've gone far beyond gentle laugh production, on into advanced practical jokes. Which are certainly not practical. Some would even question whether they actually fall into the joke category. As a result of my membership in this cluster of certifiable nuts, my bathroom was once filled with balloons (floor to ceiling); my living room furniture was moved out, and a beach—complete with two tons of sand—moved in. Two live chickens were delivered to the back of my car. And forty-six bowling balls were sent to my house.

Yes, bowling balls. Doug and I were in the process of moving from Philly to Boston. I had to go to Seattle to settle my mother's estate. Consequently I wasn't available to finish our packing, and our generous friends Donna and Fred volunteered to help. I should have been suspicious, but noooo! . . . I assumed they were just trying to be good Samaritans. This, of course, was a mistake.

The wind was howling the day we arrived in Boston—a strong nor'easter had hit the area. Doug was at his parents' with our baby girl and I was freezing in the back of the moving truck, telling the movers where to take boxes and crates. Some were clearly marked, some were not. They kept bringing me heavy, odd-shaped boxes, asking, "Where does this one go?" I opened one to discover a sparkly red bowling ball.

I don't bowl. I have never owned a bowling ball. In frustration I told them to put it in Sonny's bedroom. A few minutes later they brought me a box labeled "kitchen pots and pans."

"This one's really heavy," the muscled moving man told me. "Are you sure it goes in the kitchen?" Again I took their razor knife and cut the tape. Inside I found my pots and pans, and *two* bowling balls. Now I moved from frustrated to fuming. I thought, When did Doug start collecting bowling balls, and why in the world did he pack them in the kitchen stuff?

Next came our furniture. The movers attempted to lift Sonny's chest of drawers, and we were all startled by a loud banging. My hands were freezing but I managed to pull the bottom drawer open. I had emptied it myself and packed the contents in a box, so I had no clue what could be making such a racket. Inside a dark blue bowling ball with delicate white marble swirls glowed in the stormy light. It was kept company in the drawer by a traditional bowling ball of coal black. I started to chuckle, then burst into hysterical laughter, realizing that Donna and Fred's kind offer to help had contained a hidden motive.

By the time we had finished unpacking in Boston a few weeks later I had discovered forty-six bowling balls. They were stuffed in boxes labeled "attic," "basement," and "master bedroom," even in one box marked "linens."

What does one do with forty-six bowling balls, especially when one doesn't bowl? Good question. It took me weeks to come up with the right answer. Then, one day, sitting on the edge of the bathtub scrubbing out a scummy soap ring, it hit me. I ran screaming down the stairs, "Janey, get me my paints!"

My husband, Doug, and roommate, Jane, watched in confusion as I started to paint bowling balls. I knew many of Fred and Donna's business associates and friends. It was February, the season for Valentine's greetings. So, on one I painted "You Auto Be My Valentine. Love, Donna," and I boxed it up to send to her mechanic. To one business associate who held a high-level position at a cable shopping network, I wrote, "You don't have to shop for a Valentine . ... be mine. Love, Donna." For the curator of the Brandywine River Museum, a highly respected member of the art community in Chadds Ford, Pennsylvania, I painted a picture of Andrew Wyeth's famous model

Helga on a bowling ball, with this note: "You Art to Be My Valentine. Love, Donna."

Fred was vacationing with his family in Hawaii, so I custom-painted a ball for each member of his family, including his dignified and stoic father. I chuckled as I painted a picture of his teenage son riding a surfboard, imagining Fred's family lugging their thirteen-pound bowling balls onto the plane home.

I placed each completed masterpiece back into its original box and attached FedEx shipping labels. Now, the coup de grâce—I had Janey call Donna and joke about the bowling ball caper. Donna was so proud of herself, she bragged how she and Fred had pulled the entire joke off without a hitch, and how it hadn't cost them a cent since a bowling alley had donated abandoned balls for their hoax. Smugly I took the phone from Janey as I was wrapping the unique, if heavy, Valentines.

"D-ster, what are you doing?" Donna asked when she heard the sound of strapping tape being ripped off its roll.

"Oh, I'm just fixing a box to send to my sister for Valentine's Day," I lied. Then I whined, "I just hope she gets it in time."

She took the bait. "Here, let me give you my FedEx number and you can send it to her overnight."

I thanked her profusely and carefully wrote the number on the box I was wrapping. Then I wrote it on the forty-five other boxes crowding my living room floor. And then I called FedEx!

I'm not the only one who receives gifts of laughter from her children. This listener, Beth, shares one of those times with us.

I'm learning what life is about from my three-and-a-half-year-old daughter. It's to be spent with loved ones. My husband was out of town for a week and we had the best time. Saying our prayers each night, we always "Thank God for Mommy, Daddy, and our dog, Murphy." Then I'll say, "Who else?" and Katelyn will add other friends and relatives. Well, my cousin has a dog named Bud, and Katelyn is very fond of him. One night, when I asked, "Who else?" she would say, "Bud." And giggle. Then I'd add, "And Grandpa and Grandma, and who else?" And she'd say, "Bud," and giggle. We got to laughing so hard our stomachs and faces hurt. I keep moments like this close to me, just as I paste photographs in albums. I want to remember Katelyn's laughter always.

When Sonny was little he loved to go on adventures. We would put on coats and boots and head out the door, hand in hand. "Clean up your room, and then we'll go," I chided. "You have to help me," he begged. So together we tossed his toys, one by one, into his toy box, and soon we were off on our adventure.

One particular spring day we decided to go to Lincoln Park. There is a rock beach where at low tide you can turn the stones over to find tiny sand crabs and hermit crabs scurrying away. Two-year-old Sonny stationed himself a few feet from the water's edge and began picking up rocks, one at a time, and hurling them with all his strength into the water. He wasn't interested in catching crabs or picking up shells. *Kerplunk, kerplunk* went each rock with a satisfying splash.

After an hour or so I took his cold wet hand and tried to lead him back to the car. He'd pull away and toss another rock. Finally my tone became insistent. "Sonny, we have to go. Mommy has to go to work."

"No, Momma," he said firmly. "I'm not done yet."

"Done with what?" I shouted in frustration.

"I'm helping God clean up his room," he said, and heaved another rock into the sea.

A Time to Mourn

When I was a young woman and I heard the term "mourn," I pictured thin-waisted women attending a funeral in severe black dresses, wearing small hats with veils over their pained faces, like movie stars on our ancient black-and-white TV. Because I had never actually lost someone I dearly loved, I figured the mourning process ended after the soggy casseroles were eaten (or not) and the Pyrex baking dishes went back to the person whose name was written on masking tape on the bottom. I have since discovered that a funeral is to mourning what lovemaking is to a baby: only the beginning of a very, very long process. And mourning, I've discovered, is not an emotion reserved for death and dying. It wears myriad faces, as does its counterpart, rejoicing.

There are a million reasons we mourn, and a million ways we do it. Some cry uncontrollably, some scream and writhe in pain, others wrap themselves up like a cocoon and shut out the world. I believe mourning is as necessary to the soul's well-being as sleeping is for our bodies. If we don't allow ourselves to mourn the many losses in our lives, we end up falling head-long into a state of depression. There is a reason that God gave us tear ducts and connected them to our hearts. They are like the pressure valve on my mother's antique pressure cooker—they keep us from exploding from the pain of loss.

Every person who has ever spent a sleepless night worrying about a child has had to mourn to some degree. Of course, mourning the loss of a child whose chubby little feet are now bigger than yours—and are walking out the door into an uncertain world—is different from mourning because their once tiny toes have decided to stomp out the door and down the path of alcohol and rebellion and drugs. And to lose a prodigal child who chooses the wild life and drug abuse is certainly different from losing a child because the drugs prescribed by the doctors are no longer effective, and a precious heart ceases to beat.

To mourn a child you have lost to death is different from mourning a child you have simply lost, a child who is suddenly missing without a trace. No ends to tie up, no quiet spot to place a rose and sit until sunset and scream at God.

And even if you aren't a parent, there are still a thousand losses to mourn. The loss of a lover, a partner, a friend. Losing a parent, a sister or a brother, a job, a pet, a home, or a marriage . . . When relationships fall apart we are left with hearts full of memories. Once you mourn the loss, those memories can bring you great joy, like the memory of a rose in the depths of a frozen winter. But in the midst of the loss, memories are like the thorns on a rose stem, piercing your soul and causing you to bleed.

I have heard it said that divorce is not tragic just because it tears two people apart, but because it is the death of a dream. Dreams are hard to mourn; they aren't tangible. How do you express, "I miss the holidays we will never share," or, "I ache for the sunsets we will never watch together"? When my first marriage ended in divorce I mourned the fact that my son would not have his dad around to teach him how to carve a car for the pinewood derby. I ached for the secret language we had developed between the two of us, the code words and expressions that were unique to our marriage. I didn't really miss him; we hadn't spent any quality time together in the last few years. I missed the dream that one day we would pose for a family portrait, children and grandchildren gathered around us.

When my brother disappeared, many years ago, we had no answers, no evidence that he and his wife were dead. So I held on to hope, praying for a miracle, all the while knowing he was gone. Once their remains were found I was able to let go of the impossible and grab hold of reality, and I had to allow myself to mourn.

Since then I have mourned a great many losses. Almost as hard as mourning is watching someone I love struggle through it. I watched my mother wrestle with the reality that her firstborn would never be in her arms again. As a mother I have not had to bury a child. I pray I never do. But for now I will watch as they pull away from my protective arms and strive to find their own way. I will mourn their growing up, and I will rejoice that I have the privilege to do so.

There is no sad time in life that doesn't contain at least a hint of hope. It doesn't appear immediately when you're mourning a great loss, but if you look for it, it's there. And sometimes, as on Nicole's saddest day, hope finds you.

I was in the eighth grade when I met Beth—this girl who sat in front of me with her long hair. I kept moving it off my desk and she'd just grin. We quickly became friends. Beth

was bright and sunny and fun to be around. We were friends all through high school. We had the same dreams; we both wanted to become teachers. She was the one who helped me get through my rough times, and I helped her through hers. We laughed and cried together. She could always get me to smile.

In May of 1999, just four days before graduation, Beth was killed. A young dump truck driver ran a red light. He didn't even brake until he hit Beth's car.

We had planned for years: we would sit next to each other at graduation—how neat would that be? It was natural—our names were next to each other in the alphabet.

We buried Beth on graduation morning. At the funeral one family member described her as a butterfly—the way she lightly flew through their lives, bringing color and happiness to everyone.

That evening at graduation I sat, numb, next to an empty chair. It was a warm spring night and the auditorium doors had been left open to catch any possible breeze. Suddenly, during one of the speeches, something caught my eye and I turned toward the side door of the hall. A yellow butterfly was drifting in through the open doorway. It fluttered along the rows of graduates, then hovered. Now it darted into my row, and to my astonishment, it landed on Beth's empty chair. I sat motionless. It stayed there only a moment, slowly moving its delicate wings, then it flitted away, above our heads now, and hovered above the stage, and finally flew out the opposite side door.

I felt I was going to cry. But then I stopped, and realized: Just like Beth . . . finding a way to make me smile.

My friend Benny Mardones, the recording artist who sang "Into the Night," sent me his experience with mourning, and the support he got from an unexpected source.

I was eighteen years old and stationed in Europe aboard the USS *Springfield,* the flagship of the Sixth Fleet. I was scared, excited, alone, never left alone, homesick, glad to be out of my one-horse town, confused, and generally hanging on by my fingernails and wit.

My dreams of rock and roll stardom were put on hold when I graduated from high school. The Vietnam War was raging and the vibe in my little Southern town was that if you were a man, you served your country in time of war; and those who didn't or went to college first to avoid the draft were looked upon differently forever.

So I went, and there I was in Europe, and the reason I hadn't adjusted yet or gotten into a groove was because I was antiauthority. I grew up hanging on street corners and thought of myself as a tough guy. Nobody told me what to do. Well, as you can imagine, I was always in trouble or on report for insubordination. Even when I obeyed an order, it was with an attitude.

I remember the morning like it was yesterday. I walked into the radio shack to start my eight hours of duty. It was seven o'clock and when I walked in I saw Chief Sullivan, and next to him was the ship's chaplain. I knew something was wrong but I was afraid to speak. The chaplain said, "Son, I have some bad news for you. Your grandfather passed away last night. We thought you'd like to fly home on emergency leave."

"No, no, no. This isn't happening," I said. "Not my grandpa." Grandpa was the only father I'd had. He was the toughest guy at the steel mill. His arms were like granite, his hands stronger than those of anybody I ever knew. When he hugged me, I was safe from the world. He was the patriarch of our family. He couldn't die. Not with me eight thousand miles away.

I left immediately on a plane out of Nice headed to Italy to catch a plane stateside. I had to see him before they buried him. I had to. My mom said the funeral was to be on Friday, and it was already Wednesday. I said, "Momma, please wait for me." She said, "Sweetheart, we'll try, but Friday they have to have the funeral."

I arrived in Italy empty inside but for anger at the cards I had been dealt. The navy, I thought. The navy sucks! I ain't never taking another order, ever. If it wasn't for the navy, I'd have been home and Grandpa somehow would still be alive. I was young, scared, and didn't know what I was thinking. Then a petty officer approached me and said, "Seaman Mardones, you've been bumped off your MATS flight—officers from NATO headquarters flying out to Washington. Sorry, we'll try to get you out tomorrow."

"But I'm on emergency leave," I yelled. "My grandpa's dead. I gotta see him. Please!"

"Sorry," he said, "Nothin' I can do."

I slumped down by my duffel bag and, without shame, just started crying.

Suddenly I heard a voice say, "Son, you all right?" I looked up and it was a lieutenant commander.

"My grandpa died and they're burying him tomorrow and I ain't gonna make it. I got bumped and I'm nobody and . . . just forget it." I put my head down and cried. He patted my shoulder and when I looked up a moment later he was standing at the counter with a bunch of other officers, and then the same petty officer was coming over to me.

"Mardones," he said, "that officer over there just gave up his seat to Washington for you. So get on board, and good luck!" I turned to the officer. I started to sputter and stammer, and then I just hugged him. The other officers looked stunned, to say the least, but he put his arms around me and hugged me back, and said, "Good luck, son." His name was Paul Gleason and he was from Cincinnati. That's all I remember, but I never looked at officers or people in positions of authority the same ever again. I made it to the funeral by a heart-beat, but in time to tell my grandpa that he was my hero and that I loved him.

When I became a rock star, in the eighties, I headlined an arena in Cincinnati, and I remember sitting up calling every Gleason in the phone book trying to find Paul Gleason, because I wanted to thank him and hug him one more time for the moments his generosity gave me with the greatest man I ever knew. I never found him, but maybe someone who knows him will read this story and tell him how much it meant to me.

Benny

Life is never simple—great joy can arrive in the midst of tragic loss and mourning. You can feel both at the same time, as I learned only too well, nursing my daughter as my mother slipped away. MaryBeth learned this even more intensely, when she experienced death and birth at the same moment.

I want to tell you about a special time in my life. The story is sad, but it is very special to me. One December morning three years ago, my children and I were rushing around, getting ready for our day—my girls were busy dressing for school. I was preparing for work. I was eight and a half months pregnant at the time.

My daughter Alyssia was very excited that morning because she was going to give some Christmas presents to friends at school. She wanted to wear her new Christmas socks and she must have changed her clothes three times trying to get just the right look. This, of course, made her late and she was afraid that she would miss the school bus. She threw on her coat and grabbed her backpack to head out the door, when I called her back. She looked at me and said she would be late. And I said, "Oh, well, then I'll just have to drive you to school." Alyssia laughed and came back up the stairs and I gave her a great big hug. I can still see her beautiful, bright brown eyes smiling up at me. We were so happy. I looked down at her and said, "I love you so much." She was so happy and squeezed me tight. I looked at her and said, "You take care of you, because I don't know what I'd ever do without you." She gave me a kiss and bounced out the door to the bus. I can still see her dancing across the yard.

I never saw those beautiful brown eyes smile at me again. That afternoon at school Alyssia was severely injured in an accident. She never regained consciousness. I sat by her bed for thirty days and only left her side when the time came to give birth to Alyssia's baby sister.

Alanna was born on Christmas Day 1996, while her sister lay critically injured only a few floors away. I welcomed one life as I let another go.

Looking back, despite my grief I am so glad I had those special moments with my Alyssia that early morning, just before she left home for the last time. It is that vision of her happy eyes that I carry in my heart every day. I know that Alyssia is always with me and in my heart. I know that she knows I never left her.

I live each day constantly reminded of God's perfect timing. At the very moment I was overcome with the searing pain of losing Alyssia forever, I was consumed by the joyous pain of bringing a new life into the world.

BROWN-EYED BOY

Where did you go,
my brown-eyed boy,
with your pockets full of rocks and string,
your head full of dragons and dreams?
When did you stop believing I was a god
and find your faith in the real one?

Where did you go,
my curly-locked boy,
with your innocent smile
and your silly songs
and trees you climbed to reach the stars?
When did you grow taller than I
and discover answers on your own?

Where did you go,
my Sonny-boy,
my precious child so filled with grace?
When did this young man appear
and suddenly take your place?
When did my kiss cease to ease the pain
and my songs start to sound out of tune?

Where did you go,
my baby boy?
Your momma misses you.

Delilah

A Time to Dance

"Mom, you are your most *white* when you dance."

My African-American teenage daughter and I were in the kitchen listening to her CDs and I was getting down with my bad self . . . or so I thought. Like Steve Martin in *The Jerk*, I lack rhythm. I don't know how to ballroom dance, I don't line dance, square dance, belly dance, ballet dance, or hip-hop.

I had dreams of becoming a famous performer when I was a little girl. I would close my eyes and picture my name in lights. I longed to stand on a brightly lit stage, hearing throngs of people applaud and cheer. The only problem is, I can't sing a note, I can't act, and I can't dance. Kinda hard to be a Broadway star, given these limitations. Oh well, I can still hop around my kitchen doing the funky chicken with my kids.

When Sonny, my firstborn, was about six he became enthralled with the Boston Ballet's performance of *The Nutcracker*. Because I worked at a radio station that sponsored the event, we got free tickets. Sonny *loved* the Rat King. He loved it so much he begged me to go back. Again. And again. Four times we went in one holiday season. If I never see those stupid Sugarplum Fairies flit about the stage again, it will be too soon.

I have marveled at Michael Jackson's moon walk and thrilled at old Fred Astaire movies. I saw *Footloose* three times when it was in the theaters and *Dirty Dancing* as many times on video. As a child I watched *The Lawrence Welk Show* to see the lovely couples glide among the bubbles.

In college I donned disco dresses and high heels and hit the nightclubs more times than I would ever admit to my mother. I thought I was pretty cool on the dance floor, spinning and posing and showing my legs. Now I can't even wear high heels, let alone dance in them.

When we lived in Philly we attended a messianic synagogue. There I was blessed to witness traditional Jewish dances performed to hauntingly beautiful worship music. The men, women, and children would form a circle, dip and kick, turn and sway, lifting holy hands to ancient rhythms, worshiping Yahweh, the God of Abraham, Isaac, and Jacob. Four thousand years their ancestors have been dancing these dances, perhaps longer.

By far the most profound and moving dance I have ever seen was on a huge video screen at a women's conference I attended. The speaker, Joni Erickson Tada, is a paraplegic; she was injured as a teenager and her once athletic body is now confined to a wheelchair. Joni has devoted her life to sharing her faith and helping others. One of her projects is to collect used wheelchairs, crutches, and leg braces. She has a team of people who refurbish them and then distribute them to third world countries. She showed a video of one of her trips to South Africa, where thousands have been wounded or maimed by land mines. On the video, Joni was distributing the medical equipment. Instead of sadness, bitterness, or rage, the bright faces seemed to glow with love, and they began to beat their fists upon the ground in time with their singing, and then they began to dance, using their arms as if they were legs, even pushing off the ground and leaping into the air for joy. I learned a lot that day about the essence of dance. It isn't about having perfect rhythm or knowing all the right moves. It's flying without wings.

If we watch for opportunities, even if our culture doesn't offer a lot of them, we can dance through life. My friend the recording artist John Tesh wrote to me about a magical dancing moment.

My wife, Connie, was on a rare business trip, and Prima and I were left to fend for ourselves. It was an adventure for her; she knew she would get to stay up late and probably eat some nasty concoction at breakfast time (although I am sure she truly believed she might starve to death).

Well, Connie and I have a dance lesson scheduled each Tuesday evening . . . for our "date night." I decided I could keep my daughter with me and take the lesson by myself. (Be careful here, real men do take dance lessons!) So I invited Prima to go with me. She was happy and excited, and I figured I was an extremely smart dad—that my daughter would find watching grown-ups dance from the sidelines fascinating and I would be acclaimed the master of multitasking. But when we were ready to leave the house, there she was—pink tutu, tap shoes, and a big smile. I thought, Oh, no, what is this going to be?

I soon found out. This little six-year-old princess participated in the dance lesson with her dad that night. She held my hands. She stood up straight. She struggled to get her little arms around me, and she looked me in the eye while she concentrated so awfully hard on each step that the instructor gave us. She danced. I spent the evening learning how to appreciate just being in a moment that was so special for my daughter and an even greater joy for her dad.

This will always be our "first dance." And when I finally have to give her away on someone else's dance floor, it will be that first dance I'll be remembering and that little girl in my arms. Pink tutu, tap shoes, and a big smile.

John

I would pick him up, he would giggle, and I'd swing his chubby legs onto my hip. Then we'd strike a seriously theatrical pose—cheeks pressed together, arms outstretched, hands clasped—and we would dance dramatically across the living room floor. When we reached the far end of the room, I would bend forward, dipping him backward until his head nearly touched the carpet. Then I'd pull him up; we'd switch arms and tango back across the room. Sometimes we danced to songs on the radio, but more often than not we sang our own songs as we danced.

Sonny was only two when we began our tango tradition, and as he grew we carefully preserved this silly practice. Out of the blue he would come and grab my hand, thrust out his arm; I would snatch him up, and together we'd march across the floor, my baby boy and me.

And then he was too big to sit on my hip, and so I'd drop to my knees and we would prance off, cheek-to-cheek. And then he grew too big for my knee walk, and I'd bend down to meet his tender face. And then he grew too big to dance. Or so I thought . . .

One day I heard singing and giggling echoing through the quiet house, coming from my daughter's bedroom. I tiptoed to the door and peeked in. There was my tall, lanky son, down on his knees. On his left arm sat his two-and-a-half-year-old sister, her cheek pressed to Sonny's, their arms outstretched.

With tears in my eyes I watched as he danced her across the floor, leaned forward ever so gently to dip her, then swept her up, and tangoed back toward the door.

Too big to tango with Mom, perhaps, but not too grown-up to preserve a family tradition.

So many important memories start out as ordinary moments. Even the simplest experience can give us tremendous joy when love plays a part. Emily, my listener, shares this special dance with her husband-to-be.

I'll never forget the night we first danced to "our song." I hadn't known this man to be unusually romantic about anything. We had made dinner together and I was doing the dishes when he came up behind me. He put his arms around

my waist and held me tight. He turned me around, grabbed my hand, and pulled me into the other room.

I wondered what was going on. He turned the lights down low and pressed play on the stereo. He pulled me close and we danced together. The song was George Strait's "I Cross My Heart." There we were, me with my wet hands from the dishes, him holding me tight and singing to me. We sang along for as long as we could until we both started to cry from all the emotions we felt. I have tears in my eyes right now just thinking about it. I will never forget how everything felt so incredibly right at that moment. That song will be played for our first dance at our wedding, and I can't wait to relive the moment, knowing he has become my husband.

A dance isn't always a romance between people falling in love. As Marjorie shows us, sometimes the best dances are the ones we dance with someone who's known us forever.

*W*hen the Second World War ended, my brother came home from serving in the navy. I was in my first year of high school and the prom was being held that week. Like any young girl, the high school prom was very important to me, but I didn't expect to attend because I didn't have a date. Then my brother offered to escort me to the dance. I was very pleased and eager to show him off to my friends. He was so handsome in his uniform.

As we entered the gymnasium, I saw that there were other servicemen there. One of the men had been drinking and was having trouble with his balance; he stood before me and asked me to dance. I was young and inexperienced and I didn't know how to say no. I didn't want to say no to a brave soldier who had just returned from a terrible war, but I was scared. It was an awkward moment as the young soldier swayed back and forth before me. He was just reaching out to grab my arm, and I was wondering how I would escape when the dance ended, when I saw my brother out of the corner of my eye. He stepped out of the crowd of couples around us and said, "Hey, sis, this is my dance, don't you remember?" He gave the soldier a big grin and danced me away to safety. I hugged him tight. I felt so protected and pleased that he was there for me. I will always remember that night as a proud young girl dancing with the bravest, smartest, best-looking man at the prom.

Here's a request I received one night from a listener named Leslie. I was touched, and I know you will be, too.

$\mathscr{I}$'m writing to request a song from you in memory of my brother, Ben. On July 15, 1999, he lost his battle with cancer. He was only twenty. Over the course of six years, he went through three surgeries, radiation, and several types of chemotherapy. He also endured a period of time when extreme depression alternated with rages that caused him to lash out and kick holes through doors. Illness and learning disabilities caused him to fall a year behind in high school, and he watched most of his friends drift away. He was never able to learn to drive or have a steady job, due to the constant tiny seizures that were only partly controlled by medication.

Despite all of this, Ben never lost his crazy sense of humor or his love of life. He was the first one to want to go out and do anything, and he always had some joke or pun ready to make the rest of us laugh. Ben also had very interesting musical tastes. His favorite musicians were "Weird Al" Yankovic and Phil Collins. In his last few weeks, as Ben slowly slipped away, my parents played this music for him. The last song they played on the morning my brother died was "Dance into the Light," by Phil Collins. On the first anniversary of his death, would you play this song for me in memory of my brother, and for all the people out there who have gone through or are going through this now? I think that Ben would have wanted to tell people the message conveyed in this song—life is too short to be worried about the bad stuff. That way, when the end comes along, you can leave with no regrets—dancing all the way.

It was a night like any other night. I was tired as I drove home from work, thinking about all the things that must be attended to before I could turn in. I pulled up behind our house, grabbed my bag, and got out of the car. As I started to walk in, I happened to look up. In an instant I forgot the worries of the busy day and stood in awe . . .

I had never seen a night sky quite so spectacular. A high, fluffy covering of clouds spanned the sky, east to west, north to south. The clouds were illuminated in the strangest way; you could see the edge of each and every one, glowing an ethereal silvery white. There was a single break in the blanket above, a huge hole in the middle of the sky, and through it the full moon was glowing, a brilliant, perfect white orb among the clouds, and it was surrounded by a rainbow, a colorful halo glowing in the night.

I stood in our backyard, gazing upward, and the words to an old King Harvest tune started ringing in my head: "Dancing in the Moonlight." I ran into the house, dropped my bag, and went to find Doug. I had romantic notions playing in my head of a midnight dance under the spectacular sky. I found him sleeping soundly in our bed (he is less than friendly when he is sleeping) and I tried to wake him. After several unsuccessful attempts, I gave up and walked out. I felt angry and rejected, my feelings hurt that he wouldn't jump up and enjoy my romantic fantasy with me.

I walked into our little kitchen and looked out once again upon the beauty in the heavens . . . the moon was still shining, the rainbow was still glowing in a perfect circle around it, the clouds were still tinged with silver. I could not stand there and let the beauty escape, so I zipped up my coat and headed out to the backyard again. I stood there, frozen in the beauty of the moment, yet still feeling a bit sorry for myself.

I uttered a small prayer of praise, thanking the Almighty for this wonderful scene. And then, in a voice that was so clear it was almost audible, I heard God speak to my heart. "I didn't create this moment for you and Doug," He seemed to say. "I created it for you and me." And together we danced in the moonlight.

A Time to Embrace

My mom was over six feet tall. Her hands were as big as a man's. When she hugged you, you knew you were hugged! She had an annoying habit of hugging and kissing her children whenever she said good-bye. I don't mean good-bye as in, I'm leaving for a week or a month. She hugged and kissed us when we went out the door for school, when she went out the door to run errands. When I was a toddler that was fine, but by the time I reached junior high it was rather embarrassing to have Mom hugging me as I jumped out of our beat-up oxidized red Ford Falcon station wagon in my cheerleader uniform. My grandma McGowne was equally annoying;

she not only hugged and kissed me, she insisted on calling me by my childhood nickname, "Sissy Nay-nay," regardless of who was around.

When I was three or four years old, we lived on a farm. I went with Mom to visit our neighbor's aged mother, who also lived on the farm. Grandma Mikulecky spoke only a little English. Her house smelled like biscuits and sweet tea and the brambly honeysuckle that covered the roof of her tiny cottage, which looked like something out of one of my storybooks. She had a big, black cast iron stove in the middle of her diminutive kitchen. Her family raised chickens and geese and ducks, at least a dozen different varieties of fowl.

Earlier that week a hen had been killed by a raccoon and so Grandma Mikulecky brought the tiny chicks into the house and was keeping them warm in a wooden box behind the stove. She took them out for me to see, and left me alone with the soft fluffy chicks as she went about fixing a snack.

By the time she and Mom came to check on me, three of the chicks lay lifeless on the floor. They were so sweet, so adorable and soft, I wanted to hug them. I didn't realize how hard I was hugging them. Grandma Mikulecky quickly swooped them up, saying they were sleepy and needed more rest. It wasn't until many years later that Mom told me what really happened.

I have since had to learn that you can't hold on to the ones you love too tightly. But like my mother and my grandmother, I love to hug, to embrace, to show affection by enveloping another in my arms and gently holding them close. I will always embrace the folks I love, strangers that God brings into my path, the faith that I believe in, and the dreams that I cherish.

It's surprising sometimes how a simple hug can transform your whole outlook. Many times when I'm tired or frustrated, Doug will wrap me in his muscular arms, or my baby will hug my leg with his tiny ones, and my heart is rejuvenated.

One night a woman named Kathy called my show. Like so many of my listeners, Kathy is a single mom working long, exhausting hours to support her two daughters. She shared how a few moments of closeness with them gave her the perspective she needed.

My girls are seven and nine. We have pretty hectic days, trying to get all of us ready for work and school and out the door. At times I feel like I'm just going through the motions of living. One night, the girls were tucked in bed for the night and I couldn't sleep, so I was sitting on the couch in the living room in the dark, just listening to the quiet; a rare thing, I assure you. Before I knew it, without a sound, my daughters had come and curled up on each side of me. With a sigh, in barely a whisper, I heard, "We love you, Mommy." All the long hours working, worrying about bills, feeling guilty that I can't be with them more just faded away.

I've learned not to take much of anything for granted in this life. Not a job, not a relationship, not time spent with a loved one. Fortunately, Dorothy, a listener who is a college student, is a person who is paying attention to her life. One day in particular, being wide awake to every passing moment served her well.

The day was amazingly normal. I got back from my freshman journalism class around two-thirty on that Wednesday afternoon. I remember the weather was warm for a February day. I was sitting in my dorm room watching TV when the phone rang. "Hi Honey."

"Dad! What's up?" He told me that he was passing through the area on his way home from a business trip—and he couldn't drive by without stopping in to see me. What a great surprise!

A few minutes later, I ran downstairs to meet him in the lobby. He was wearing his usual khakis and a simple dress shirt. I had already changed into my afternoon comfort outfit—warm-up pants and a T-shirt. I gave him a huge hug, giving no thought to the people all around us, some of whom might smirk at a grown-up college student hugging her dad. We sat on one of the lobby benches—since my room was not exactly "guest-worthy." I asked him about his trip, he asked me about my classes.

He also asked me how I was feeling—he jokingly accused me of giving him my pneumonia (since he had recently been experiencing mysterious chest pains). We found a phone and I helped him decide whether to order flowers or a plant to be sent to his mom for her birthday the next day. We decided on a plant—plants last longer, and time is important. I didn't realize how important it could be.

Dad and I visited for a little longer, and then he decided that he needed to get back on the road. I put my arm around his waist and walked out to the car with him. Then he gave me the greatest gift possible. He gave me a big hug, the kind where I was completely engulfed in his arms, and he said, "I'm so glad I have a daughter like you." I will be forever grateful to him for saying that, because it gave me the chance to tell him how lucky I felt to have a father like him.

So, the day that had seemed so normal, only an hour earlier, turned into the most special day I have experienced in my eighteen years. My dad's gift of those precious few minutes was the greatest gift he could give—and the last one he'd give me. He died two days later, three weeks after his fifty-third birthday, of unexpected heart problems. That visit was my last with him, but I will always treasure it, knowing our last words were words of love.

There are so many different kinds of hugs. When I held Sonny for the first time, it was one kind of embrace. When I come home from a trip, a hug (and a kiss!) from Doug is an entirely different variety. Hugging a listener, an old friend, or my littlest one when he's crying . . . each embrace is special and unique. My listener Rachael wrote to me about an embrace that encompassed a lifetime.

My brother, Todd, is in the army and we don't get to see him very often. I raised my brother, because my mother was ill. It was hard, but my brother actually turned out OK, even though I was still a child myself when I was trying to help him grow up. Because of what we went through as children, much too much to tell you about here, we have forged an extremely close bond, one that is stronger than a lot of other brother-and-sister relationships.

So it was with some sadness, but a lot of pride, that I watched my brother enlist in the army when he graduated from high school. He has quickly risen through the ranks and I'm very proud of him.

In July of last year, my grandmother passed away. We

called Todd through the Red Cross and he was allowed to come home on leave. It was not the kind of visit we had wanted, but we made the best of it. With our mother, we went to Six Flags and the zoo, and tried to have a good time despite the circumstances.

His time to leave drew nearer and it was decided that I would take him to the airport. Waiting for him to board the plane, we talked and laughed a lot about the characters we saw walking around. Then, all of a sudden it was time for him to go. I got up to hug him and truly thought I wouldn't cry—I hadn't been emotional all day. But as I pulled him close, I thought about our difficult lives and how this young man, who, in all honesty, should be in jail or on the streets somewhere, had become such a wonderful human being. I cried and thanked God for allowing us to be strong and get through our childhood to become the adults that we are. We hugged for about five minutes and then he patted my back and said, "Thank you. You raised me from a boy to a man. I'm stronger now and so are you. I'll see you again soon. Don't forget, you're in my heart, always." My brother had never before thanked me for trying my best to raise him when I was still trying to raise myself. I treasure that moment in the airport.

A severe storm had pushed across the eastern seaboard, wreaking havoc with flight schedules and temperaments alike. Our plane was delayed two hours, and then we were routed through Salt Lake City, where we had another layover, three hours this time. My baby boy was cutting two teeth, with the usual crankiness and fatigue that goes with being a one-year-old cutting teeth. I, of course, was feeling the usual crankiness and fatigue that goes with being the mother of a teething baby. All I wanted to do was go home and go to sleep.

To my delight I discovered a small, dingy lounge off the lady's rest room at the crowded airport. Because my son has never fallen asleep without a fight, and because I didn't want to burden the other already exhausted travelers with a screaming baby, I took him into the lounge to rest. There was only a low, dirty blue plastic couch and a matching chair in the stale room. I took Zacky in my arms and lay down on the couch, rocking him to sleep as I screamed a lullaby. I don't know how long it had been since we had dozed off . . . I awoke to see a well-appointed lady sitting just a few inches from my head.

Somewhat startled, I started to sit up. She said, "Go back to sleep, I just came in to rest, too." I lay my head back down but turned my face toward hers. She was a beautiful woman; she looked to be in her early fifties and was carrying a black flight bag. She explained that she was on her way to Alaska to work, that she was a pilot for a small airline. She had been up all night and was exhausted. I was intrigued. I have met only one other female commercial pilot, so I started to ask her questions about her job and her life.

She said her schedule, two weeks flying, two weeks at home, allowed her to enjoy her career and gave her time at home as well. I asked her if she was married, and if her husband minded her being away half the month. Her bright blue eyes filled with tears, and she said, "He didn't mind at all . . . he was also a pilot. But now he is gone and the house is so quiet."

She went on to say he had died in his sleep while she was up changing and feeding their new grandbaby. He had been gone only a few months, and by the raw pain I heard in her voice, I knew she had just begun traveling down the path of grief.

She told how he had encouraged her to pursue her pilot's license and had helped her to get her different ratings. They had worked for the same airline for several years, commuting to their home in Texas. They saved and bought an old fixer-upper on seven acres of land. Their plan was to renovate the house together.

We talked of dogs and ducks and mending fences. She shared how some baby ducklings they had been given had started to follow an older duck they had raised, thinking it a parent. The older duck, however, was not the least bit interested in the noisy little ones, and wanted instead to follow the couple's German shepherd. The dog tolerated the duck but much preferred the company of the woman's husband. So when her husband went outside to get the mail or mend a broken fence, he was followed by a large dog, a mallard duck, and two little baby ducks, quacking as they hurried to keep up with the parade.

I checked my watch and realized my plane would be boarding soon, so I bundled Zacky up and grabbed my travel bag and started to leave. As I stood to go she asked if I was married. "Yes," I said, "We're celebrating our seven-year anniversary this weekend."

"Hold him extra long when you get home," she said, the tears back in her eyes. "Hold him all night long. . ."

For many years I nursed foolish grudges and walked around with a painted smile on my face. I was unable—or unwilling—to deal with my emotional baggage, so I tried to hide the pain. When I was twenty-seven or twenty-eight I began the difficult but necessary process of healing. It took years and a lot of tears, but with God's help and lots of support, I let go of a lot of anger and hurt. Still, there are times when life is overwhelming. One of my greatest blessings is the strength and comfort my husband, Doug, gives me so unselfishly. I wrote this poem for him when we were first married.

Curled up on the couch,
my feet tucked under you,
and yours
    under me.
I gaze at the oak mantle
desperately in need of dusting.
The beautiful roses
you bought to surprise me
have blossomed,
the petals are scattered,
along with Sonny's spilt popcorn,
on the floor.

I think about jumping up
and being productive.
I think about
unanswered fan letters,
unpaid bills,
unwashed dishes,
unbaked pies,
and then I think about a lonely old lady,
her face dried up,
her house spotless,
even the top
of the refrigerator.

But no one notices.

No one goes to see her ordered life,

she doesn't want it cluttered.

I lay back my head,

smile at the rose petals,

gaze into your eyes,

and tuck my feet further under.

Delilah

A Time to Refrain from Embracing

'*ve never let go of anything that didn't have claw marks all over it."

I don't recall when I first heard that quote, or even who said it. I just remember chuckling at how applicable it was to my own life. Whether it's a relationship, a job, a city, a dream, or even the twenty extra pounds I gained during my pregnancies, I have a difficult time just opening my arms wide and letting go. It comes naturally to some people, like breathing. I watch in wonderment as people I know and love go through the process of letting go with grace, ease, even dignity. Not so with me. I scream and rage and cry and kick and try to manipulate situations so that I can have my own way. I try to bargain with God, especially when the thing that needs to be let go is a person, someone I love who is dying . . . Please, God, if you will heal them I promise to tell everyone I meet about your kindness and mercy. Please, God, if you just let me keep this job, I promise to show up earlier and stay later and work harder. Please, God, if you'll just help my friend and me work out our differences and put our friendship back together I won't eat any Cadbury eggs for a year.

I'm great at embracing, holding on, and squeezing tight. I am not so good at standing back and feeling at peace with knowing there are some situations that call for letting my arms drop to my sides.

When I was a young woman I married an African-American man, and for doing so I was banished from my father's family. I tried everything in my power to convince them to see things my way. I sent cards and boxes of chocolate-covered cherries at Christmas. I wrote long letters explaining the lunacy of prejudice. I cried and I begged and I prayed to a God I didn't even know.

Nothing worked. Their belief system was firmly in place long before my marriage, long before my birth. Nothing I said or did would change it, and I had to accept the consequences of my decision, no matter how wrong I knew my family was.

Our marriage was volatile, to say the least. Both of us brought too much emotional baggage into the relationship, and both of us were too stubborn and prideful to admit that we needed to seek counsel or help. After a few tumultuous years we split up and began living life separately. He seemed to adjust to his new life with ease. I, however, couldn't move on. I was actually crazy with pain, trying everything to manipulate him home.

Shortly after our divorce was final he moved out of state. And shortly after he moved, I packed my car and my infant son and followed him, telling myself I just needed a short vacation. In the same city where he had moved. What a coincidence.

When I arrived, my ex-husband was surprised but seemed genuinely happy to see us. After a few days I started to believe that my trick had worked and that somehow, without facing our issues or dealing with our various addictions, we could live happily ever after. I walked into his bathroom one morning and saw a key chain with the pet name I called him engraved on it. I was thrilled. This was the evidence I needed to show that he still cared, that he still loved me! And then I picked the piece of brass up and lovingly turned it over. Engraved on the other side were the words "All my love, Enid." I set the key chain down, picked up my baby boy, packed my few bags, and left. I knew all the screaming and crying and clinging and holding in the world wouldn't repair our lives. It was time to stop trying to hold on, and I let go.

Several years later my father was diagnosed with lung disease. As he was nearing the end, he finally relented and called me. It had been over ten years since we had spoken. We actually had a wonderful conversation, for as long as his breath would allow us to talk. He wanted to give me an antique pot-bellied stove, his way, I guess, of saying I was forgiven. I refused the stove and told him all I wanted was for him to make peace with God, and to ask God's forgiveness so that we might be able to spend eternity together one day. He scoffed and said, "No thanks," before saying good-bye.

A few weeks later, he passed away. When my sister called to say Dad had just died, as she sat with him and comforted him, I was devastated beyond words. I felt we had no closure, no reconciliation. But then my little brother, Tim, got on the phone and told me that the day before, Dad had asked to speak with a minister. One was summoned through the hospice program, and Dad asked him to pray for him. Together they prayed, he asked Jesus into his heart, and my father was baptized on his bed. Less than twelve hours later he breathed his last. I didn't get to hug him and tell him good-bye; he refused to even allow me to come home and visit. But I believe that one day I will see him face-to-face, and then there will be no refraining from embracing.

One of the things I love about my job is that I get to see people who have suffered start to heal. But this is also a hard thing to watch. A listener wrote to me with a story of an unspeakable hurt she had suffered at the hands of someone she trusted. While it might seem that the way toward recovery is forcing yourself to trust again, Heather taught me that it's more important to take the time to heal. As a part of her recovery process, she decided to go public with her story. And while she knew she wasn't ready to trust a man in her life romantically, she took a risk and found a friend.

A few weeks ago, I wrote an article in my campus newspaper. I decided to let go of the shame of being a sexual abuse survivor and share the positive side of recovery. I had never received positive feedback from any males in my life about being a survivor. Several nights ago, I felt confident enough to ask a male neighbor his thoughts about my article. He said he had not had a chance to read it, but I had a copy, and to my surprise, he agreed to read it right then, in front of me.

A part of me panicked as I remembered past experiences of guys wanting nothing to do with me after I disclosed the truth about my life. Instead of allowing the doubts to resurface, I decided to pray to God that no matter what Owen's reaction was, I would not let it affect my goal . . . to be real.

The moments that followed showed me that God does answer prayers. Reading my article, Owen got tears in his eyes. No one has ever gotten tears in their eyes after knowing what I've gone through. He didn't focus on the details of abuse. Instead, he asked about the recovery process. He listened patiently. Since I have not known men who acted that way, I thought he was staying there talking to me now because I somehow made him feel obligated to me. I thanked him and tried to let him know that he was free to leave. He said calmly, "No, I'm not leaving yet."

"All right," I said, and we went on, beyond talking about my past and the article. We shared more about our interests, our lives, and our dreams. Then I was surprised yet again.

Among the things I mentioned in our conversation was that when I was a child, no one ever read to me. He said, "Why don't we have story time right now?" There aren't many twenty-year-old guys who would spend their Friday night reading children's books until two in the morning!

For a long time I thought I wasn't worthy of a guy's attention. I know now that I can be the real me and still be accepted.

If you know me, you know I don't hesitate to get involved in other people's lives. It's hard for me, sometimes, to keep from shouting, "Hello! Wake up! You're heading straight for disaster!"—even when I know the other person won't hear me, that it isn't "a time to speak" and it isn't my place. I found myself in this painful situation recently, on a beautiful, sunny day in southern California.

I was trying to make an early flight out of LAX with my two small children. We had spent the previous day at Disneyland, so we were all exhausted when the alarm clock went off at 6:40 A.M. I didn't even have time to stop and get anything for the kids to eat before we had to run helter-skelter through the airport and board our plane.

Standing in line with my baby on my hip, I noticed a tall strawberry blond at the counter talking to the ticket agent. She was obviously agitated and nervous, shifting from one high-heeled shoe to the other. Her face appeared to be close to my age, perhaps a few years younger. But her body was that of a woman in her early twenties, tight and muscular and very, very tanned. She wore an electric blue knit top and miniskirt and at least a dozen matching blue-beaded bracelets and ankle bracelets and dime-store blue sunglasses my teenage daughter would have loved.

She finally seemed somewhat satisfied with the information the ticket agent was giving her. She grabbed her oversized purse and joined us in line to board. The flight to Sacramento was short and took only about an hour. As I was slowly gathering up the kids and our carry-ons, I watched the woman nervously exit the plane and rush to collect her luggage.

I went to the baggage carousel and retrieved our suitcase, our shoulder bags, Zacky's stroller and car seat. Once I had all of our belongings I attempted to balance our mountain of stuff and take the two children outside to wait for a shuttle bus to take us to the rental car area. The nervous woman in the electric blue outfit was the last to board the shuttle bus and we chatted briefly as my car seat nearly struck another passenger as it careened off the mountain of luggage.

At the car rental counter I began to unload the kids and our various pieces of baggage. She offered to watch Shay and Zacky while I climbed back aboard the shuttle to get the cumbersome car seat. When I had our mountain of belongings piled on the sidewalk I asked her where she was headed. She said she needed to rent a car and drive to Redding, about two hours north. I told her I was headed to Redding to meet up with my husband and our other children, and I asked her if she would like to ride with us rather than rent a separate car. I don't usually offer rides to complete strangers, especially with my children in the car, but for some reason I felt compelled to ask her to make the journey with us.

She was genuinely relieved and excited, and I could tell that she had a lot on her mind. We loaded our packages and parcels into the neat, white car and headed to I-5. As I drove she started telling me what a miracle it was that I offered her the ride. She had missed an earlier flight that was to take her first to San Francisco, and then on to Redding. Because she had missed it she would have had to wait hours to catch another flight, so she opted instead to fly to Sacramento and drive the distance. She hadn't reserved a rental car, however, and she was afraid that since it was Father's Day she would end up stuck with no transportation to Redding, a city she seemed hell-bent on reaching as quickly as possible.

I could tell by the outfit and the perfume she kept putting on as she talked, she was going to meet a man. I casually asked her, "How long have you been seeing this guy?" and she looked at me with her eyes wide, and exclaimed, "You must be a mind reader!"

I wanted to say, No, but your body language is screaming that you are going to meet some man you barely know! But I restrained myself and started to ask her questions. Her name was Sharon and she had two small children. She had been divorced for six years and didn't know where their father was. He had left when they were babies and never contacted them. She lived alone with her children on four acres of land; she had a horse and had just completed her bachelor's degree. She was bright, strong, independent, and obviously loved her children. She pulled out several adorable photographs of them.

While I had no clue what was ahead for her, I could tell by her nervousness that she could use a listening ear. As she talked and I gently pried into her business, I discovered she was a very lonely woman who was on her way to Redding to meet a man named Kevin. A mutual friend had set them up and she was hoping that he would be "the one." She said she was going to Redding to see about relocating there to be closer to him.

She was giddy with excitement as she described him. She said she had never seen a photograph but they talked every day. He had two daughters, loved his children very much, and was a hard worker. She said she was tired of living alone and had come to the conclusion that she really wanted a husband to love and a man to be a father to her children. Her friend had told her he was a wonderful father to his daughters and she felt he would be an equally wonderful stepfather.

One slight problem. He was married.

I tried to pray as I drove. "Please, God," I begged, "let me have words that will open her eyes to the disastrous situation she is getting into without making her feel that I'm judging her or telling her what to do."

"What is a beautiful woman like you doing rushing into such a terrible situation?" I blurted before God could stop me.

"He should have been divorced two years ago," she said defensively. "His wife is crazy and he has only stayed for their two children." I asked how long they had been separated. "Oh, they aren't separated yet," she went on, "but he sleeps on the couch and he's filed papers."

My mind raced back some seventeen years to when I had heard those same words. When I rushed headlong into love with a married man. He did divorce his wife. He married me. And a few years later he was seeing someone else behind my back. I talked to his new friend after our divorce was final. "He told me how you were crazy and how you didn't understand him," she had said. The same words he had said to me about his previous wife. It was then that I learned the hard way that a person who cheats on a spouse will cheat on the next one.

She was convinced that she and this man were meant to be together, that the fact that I had offered her a ride was a sign. I could think of nothing to say that wouldn't end the conversation. Still, I bluntly asked if his wife knew he was going to meet another woman. She looked at me as if I had just grown a second head. "Are you kidding? She'd kill him." I had hoped she would realize that if the wife was jealous, chances were that he wasn't sleeping on the couch as he'd said, but again she wasn't eager to hear what I had to say.

We finished the drive and I pulled the rental car up outside the hotel where they were meeting. A very handsome, jovial man with a lovely smile and thick, dark hair approached our car as we got out.

"Kevin?" she shrieked and ran to his arms as I clumsily reached for her bags. I didn't know this woman, had never laid eyes on her until a few hours earlier, and yet a part of me wanted to protect her as an old friend. I wanted to snap at him, You lying jerk, it's Father's Day, why aren't you home with your precious daughters instead of here lying to your wife and using this woman who is obviously falling in love with you? But I didn't.

As I watched the two of them, this woman and her soon-to-be lover, I thought of all the things I wanted to say. I wanted to share my beliefs with her, tell her adultery was wrong, that it could only end in heartache and pain. That a relationship that begins in betrayal has no roots to help it grow, and before she knew it she'd be left alone again.

I wanted to tell her she didn't have to wear skin-tight miniskirts and a pound of makeup, that she was a beautiful, striking woman who any man would be proud to be with. I wanted to tell her that she and her children were precious and worthy of being loved by someone who would be one hundred percent committed to just them. But I knew she wouldn't hear me, and if she did hear my words, she wouldn't believe me. I knew this too painfully well. Years before, my friends had warned me of disaster ahead, and I hurried off to meet it. I knew that nothing I said could change her mind if she wasn't ready to change it.

So instead I shook Sharon's hand and told her to please know that God loved her and that He was there should she ever want to listen. And then, as I got back in the rental car and drove away, I did the only thing I could do in the situation. I prayed for a woman, prayed for a man and his wife, and prayed for four children I had never met. I prayed and I drove.

"What do you want for your birthday this year?" I asked my soon-to-be-six-year-old, Sonny. "A little brother," was his sweet reply. A great idea, except for the fact that I was a single parent at the time. The only one who wanted another child in the family more than Sonny was me. I had hoped to have at least three children by this stage of my life, but a lot of things had not turned out as I had hoped. It was just the two of us, traversing the countryside and enjoying life together. The two of us, going on grand adventures and supporting each other through life's storms. The two of us camping and hiking and swimming and biking and roller-skating and reading bedtime stories. Sonny ached for a little brother, and I wanted more children.

Finally I called an adoption agency and asked about single parent adoption. Because I had a good job and I owned my own home, I was a great candidate to adopt a special-needs child. That is a child whom others might not consider adopting because of past abuse, neglect, physical or emotional handicaps, or simply because of its race.

After many classes, a completed home study, and months of waiting, our caseworker called to say they had found a little boy who they felt would fit into our little family. I was so excited that I had taken little time for prayer. When I finally decided to seek heavenly input, my prayer was something like this: "Father, please bless my decision and make this adoption go smoothly." As I recall, the response I felt in my heart was something like this: "This is not my will for now." But being the somewhat hardheaded woman I am, I pressed on.

Peanut, as he was called, had been born prematurely. He was a beautiful African-American boy with huge black eyes and a serious little face. He was tiny at birth, not only because he was premature but because he was born crack addicted. He was one of six siblings his mother had lost to the state due to neglect and abuse. She never even took Peanut home from the hospital. Now he was seventeen months old and not much bigger than most babies at ten months.

First we saw a photograph, and then a meeting was arranged. Within two weeks we were having visitations in his foster family's home, and a week after that I was allowed to take him for weekend stays. Since he hadn't ever been named by the agency or the foster family, I chose the name Micah, but we still called him Peanut.

I had the nursery ready, the crib assembled, the room painted, the toys purchased. I bought a car seat, a stroller, a changing table. Sonny fell instantly in love with his new baby brother, and played with him for hours. All was going perfectly. Until Mother's Day weekend.

I received a call from our caseworker at the adoption agency, a tall woman who rarely smiled. She had met Doug, my new boyfriend, a few days earlier. He had called the agency to say that he was interested in pursuing a relationship with me and that he wanted to take their parenting classes, since he had never been around small children. Instead of welcoming his enthusiasm, our caseworker demanded to know what his plans were for our family. He was honest and said he wasn't completely sure, but that he hoped to be a part of my family in the future and he wanted to learn all that he could about children, since he would be spending time around Peanut. Our caseworker took one look at Doug's ponytail and noticed he was younger than me, and her already stern countenance turned to steel.

She called on Mother's Day weekend and said she was stopping by for a visit. She arrived, along with a second case-worker, and together they took Peanut from me. They said the birth mother had decided to try to clean up her act and get off drugs and that they had to place him back with the foster family until she had successfully completed a drug rehab program.

I'm afraid I was not the picture of composure. I am not a stoic person. Even though Peanut hadn't been mine for long, I had grown to love him as my own. I screamed and actually physically fought to keep him in my arms. The caseworkers left with the baby, and I collapsed.

The next several hours I spent on the bathroom floor, throwing up and writhing in pain. Friends watched Sonny and tried their best to comfort him. I prayed for strength and a release from the heartache I was experiencing. I prayed for Peanut, that his tiny little heart wouldn't be hurt. I prayed for Sonny, that he wouldn't be crushed and that this disappointment wouldn't cause future fear of intimacy or attachment. I prayed for God to do a miracle and make them change their minds. They didn't.

But God had other plans for me and for the tiny baby I had lost. Only three months later I lost my job at the radio station. Had I been allowed to keep Micah, I would not have been able to leave the state with him for up to two years, because he was a state child and not yet legally free for adoption. Because of my contract at work, I couldn't get another radio job in Boston. Since radio is all I have ever done, I don't know how I would have earned enough money to keep our house and to care for the children. Losing the baby meant I could take Sonny and move to Philadelphia for a new job.

Two years went by, and Doug and I married. Then one day, my good friend and producer, Janey, came to me, her eyes wide with joy. "Guess what, I know about Peanut," she told me excitedly. Her sister had been standing in line at a grocery store and saw an article about a disc jockey. She mentioned to the clerk that she knew a disc jockey, and told her that her little sister was Delilah's producer. The clerk was excited, because her mother had been Micah's foster mother.

She told Jane's sister that the baby I had loved had been adopted by a wonderful African-American family; the father was a doctor and the mother was a stay-at-home mom. They had never been able to conceive and they had adopted a daughter a few years before Peanut. He lived in a lovely neighborhood on the south shore of Massachusetts, in a beautiful home with his sister. He was the son they had hoped and prayed for for many years. He was safe, he was secure, and he was loved more than life, I am sure.

It was not God's plan that Peanut should be my child. If I had fought for him, refusing to give up and battling the agency, I could have damaged both our lives. I might not have been able to adopt again, and who knows where Peanut might have ended up. I had to let go of my desires and live with this loss, that a better plan for his young life, and mine, might unfold.

A Time to
Keep Silence

I've been in broadcasting for well over half my life, but I don't listen to the radio very often. I don't have a wide-screen television set. I don't have a fancy stereo. The last stereo I purchased was from a catalogue in 1978 for my first apartment. I couldn't wait to play Peter Frampton and Heart on the turntable! It came complete with an eight-track cassette player and two speakers.

My husband has a boom box he carries from room to room so he can listen to loud rock music at horrific decibels as he works around our money-pit house, but I prefer the sound of silence when I'm at home with my children. Actually, this is an oxymoron; there is no such thing as silence with my children! But at least the clamor and clatter is from them, not from some electronic source.

During the day I putter around the house, do laundry, dishes, fix dinner, or work in my garden and watch the birds as they flock to the feeder, and I do it all minus the usual noise of our modern-day society. I love the delicious repose my old house offers, the creak of the ancient hardwood floors as Shaylah dances from room to room, helping her baby brother learn to walk. I love the symphony performed by the tiny birds that visit the backyard feeder and the soft tinkle of wind chimes in the breeze.

I don't have a clock radio; I don't like to awake to noise in the morning. I don't have a TV or a radio in my kitchen; I like to listen to the bacon sizzle, the pot boil, the burger fry, the water run. I don't even like to use the dishwasher; it's too noisy for me. I prefer to stand at the kitchen sink and watch the squirrels outside as I wash our piles of plates and mismatched cups.

It's funny, I make my living talking and playing music, and yet most of the day I talk very little except to read storybooks to Shaylah and say such brilliant things as "You wanna ride da horsey?" or, "Did you do da poo poos?" and, "What's the doggie say?" to my toddler, Zacky.

On the radio, my job is to make sound and keep it coming.

In radio, silence is known as *dead air,* and it is strictly forbidden. But silence is an important part of my show—the kind of silence that means I have shut my mouth and am listening to what a listener is saying to me. As you can imagine, this isn't easy for me.

When a listener or a family member or a friend comes to me with a problem, my first impulse is to start talking and try to solve it. But I have learned to make the effort to stop myself and realize that what the person may need from me more than the benefit of my vast experience and profound wisdom is for me to just sit still and listen. So, I press my lips together and keep silent. Often, just a moment to think is all that person needs to get to the right answer—rather than *my* answer.

Living life in a noisy city near a street where sirens constantly blare, with a telephone that constantly rings, six kids who constantly argue, a husband who loves loud music, a baby who screeches and bangs pots and pans, and the nonstop stream of sound that is radio, it's hard to remember "what peace there may be in silence." But for my sanity's sake, I try. I try to be still, to listen to what God and other people are trying to tell me. I listen, and I learn.

Best friends know the value of silence. They've said everything there is to say to each other, and they've learned to listen to the voice of the heart. My listener Jaime shared this experience with us.

*W*ith graduation day getting closer and closer, my best friend and I have been having trouble even beginning to talk about what's ahead. She's the one who's graduating. She is off into the real world and I'm not. She's a college senior and I'm only a sophomore. The closer the day comes, the shorter our times together seem. And the less we seem to talk. But strangely, when I walk away I feel that we've shared the greatest conversation. Though we just spent time together walking, or sitting silent in a restaurant, or sprawled studying on the floor of her room, we've said volumes. Though we can't come up with words, our silences say so very much, and it all comes from the heart. Of all the times we've talked through the night, it's the silences I'll remember.

The sky was a thick, cold gray. The clouds looked as if they were too tired to hang in the air, so they nestled down on the sides of the mountain and gave it a mystical appearance. It had been snowing since we arrived the previous day, and the children were ecstatic.

I sit on the chairlift, wiping the snow from the cheap sunglasses I had purchased at the corner drugstore, wishing I had spent the extra money on ski goggles instead. To my right sits Sonny, my eldest. The little bit of his face that I can see above the turtleneck and beneath the ski cap is amazingly handsome and mature. Last time I sat on a chairlift with him, he barely reached my shoulder; now he towers above me. Next to him sits his brother, Manny, our newly adopted son. Their ski hats tell the story. Sonny's is light green, and it fits neatly on top of his short-cropped hair, the edges turned up. Manny's is purple, green, yellow, and blue. Like the dog's hat in the book, *Go Dog, Go,* it hangs halfway down his back. He looks like one of Santa's elves all grown up. This is his first time on a chairlift, and the joy in his face makes his dark skin glow.

We talk about everything and nothing as the chair ascends the mountain slope. Silence and snow wrap the trees beneath us, making them look like a greeting card. We lament the fact that the fog is so thick we can't see the mountain we are about to glide down. And then Sonny grabs my mittened hand and points to our left. There is a perfectly round hole in the clouds and bright blue sky is peering through. The break in the clouds is positioned so that the peak of the mountain is in the middle. For a few moments the three of us stare in silence at the mountaintop, the golden sunlight illuminating it like a painting. It is as if the scene would disappear if any of us said a word. The chairlift begins to slow and we have to hop off. We still don't speak.

Before I begin my descent, I look back up to the sky. The blue has disappeared into the thick gray and the moment is gone. The boys and I remain silent as we push off and fly down the mountain.

Jean, another of my listeners, lost her sister to leukemia a year or two ago. One of her favorite memories is of a quiet time.

*M*y sister was only forty-three years old and she died less than a month after she was diagnosed. She had a wonderful husband and three lovely girls. All of them miss her so very much.

One Sunday afternoon I was sitting with her in her hospital room. She had begun her chemotherapy and she tired easily. She climbed into bed, pulled up the covers, and asked me to read to her. I pulled a chair close to the bedside and opened *A Walk in the Woods,* a wonderful story about hiking the Appalachian Trail.

As I started to read, I balanced the book on my lap and reached over and took her hand. She let her hand rest gently in mine. I felt absolutely trusted. I looked over at her from time to time as I read, and she smiled a soft, sleepy smile that went straight to my heart. It was a sweet moment for me. My sister and I spoke volumes without saying a word.

I look out the window of the top cabin of our houseboat and see the steam rising off the lake, a magical mist. The sun is just appearing above the tree-lined hilltop, and I see reflections of fluffy clouds in the waters beneath me. I don't recall waking to such peace in years. The hills surrounding Lake Shasta are emerald green, covered with tall ponderosa pine and leafy oak. The gentle slopes that reach to the water's edge call to me to leave my warm berth and go for a hike. Gently lapping water invites me to glide our canoe on its glassy surface.

I notice movement at the lake's edge and to my amazement I see a bald eagle bathing in the clear water. Overhead, ospreys circle and dive in the morning light. One of their huge nests sits high in a tree just yards from where our boat is docked.

Slowly I ease my arm from beneath my slumbering daughter. But the dog starts to whine, and Shaylah coughs. Doug begins to grumble as I tumble over his tired body.

Though the perfectly still moment has passed, the magic of the morning sings in my heart. I thank God for allowing me to awaken to his creation.

A Time to Speak

As my mother used to tell it, I didn't actually speak until I was over two years old. I would jabber away in baby talk, and then my older brother, Matt, would translate. He understood perfectly what I wanted to say. Once I did begin to speak, though, I didn't stop. I still haven't.

After each school term, my children bring home "progress reports," or "individualized student reports." Even when they contain bad news, I feel almost proud, so affirming are these carefully worded messages from school.

When I was a kid, we got "report cards." No nonsense, just the truth in black-and-white on thin cardboard in tight little envelopes. On the card, the no-nonsense list: math, science, English, social studies, and four boxes for our grades. A to F. Simple. On the back, the teachers wrote their comments.

Every student dreaded report cards; would a grade lower than a C unaccountably appear in one of those boxes? Not me. I loved those little boxes. I loved gloating over my A's and B's.

It was the *back* of the card I hated. Without fail, the first-quarter teacher comments would be something like, "Delilah is a bright student and a delight to have in class, but she has a bit of a problem with excessive talking."

By the second quarter the language would become a little more direct: "Delilah is enthusiastic, but she tends to talk out of turn." By the end of the school year the exasperated teacher would scrawl something like, "Your daughter needs to shut up in class."

I tried. I really did. I would raise my chubby hand and wave it frantically, hoping to be the one called on each day. But sometimes I couldn't wait and I'd blurt out the answer to the question.

I have to own up: most of my talking wasn't volunteering brilliant answers. Mostly I whispered to my friends. One slight problem: unlike my friends', my voice carries. My whisper was as loud as another kid's normal speaking voice. Mrs. Brown, my second-grade teacher, even went so far as to apply a piece of duct tape over my mouth. The power of duct tape is legendary, but it met its match with me. I pushed it free with my tongue and continued whispering through it to Kelley Jacobson. The tape did, however, adhere to my long blond hair. As a result, I ended up wearing a short bob for the rest of the second grade.

When I got to junior high the teachers were waiting for me. They separated my best friends and me, knowing that if we even sat in the same homeroom we would spend all day talking. This worked only temporarily. I simply made new friends.

The year I actually got to be a member of the cheerleader squad, it wasn't because the student body voted for me; the teachers picked me, knowing my voice would be louder than anybody's, leading cheers for our miserable basketball team.

Our school awarded shiny gold pins for extracurricular activities. I wanted one in the worst way. I was still a fairly typical junior high kid, wondering who I really was, what I was good at, where I fit in. I was a show-off—that was clear. I'd do almost anything for praise, or just to be noticed.

There were a few obstacles in my path to a school pin. I wasn't compact or limber enough to make the gymnastics team. I had no musical talent, zero; so, the school band was out. No choir either; I couldn't sing a note to save my life. Even my piano teacher, Mrs. Bryant, had almost literally thrown me out.

Then the school announced a speech contest would take place. Anyone could enter. I signed up in every category. And to my delight, I won every category except one. Suddenly I became the junior high equivalent of a superstar. I collected a handful of silver dollars. And I got my school pin. It was amazing. I suddenly realized that the world had a place for people who talked too much, where the results were not sharp notes on the backs of report cards but admiration, applause, even money, not to mention the joy of joining the wearers of the school pin.

So, I had learned that there are risks when you speak out . . . risks, consequences, and rewards. And I found my calling. The contest judges, Jerome and Steve Kenegy, owned a tiny radio station in my hometown. After the contest they came up to my mother and said, "Wow, your daughter really loves to talk." This was the beginning of a wonderful thing.

The Kenegys arranged for me to report on school news and sports on the radio station; the high school set up a work-study program for me. I attended school half-day and went to the radio station the other half. I was thirteen when I delivered my first on-air school report on KDUN 1470 AM, Reedsport, Oregon.

Twenty-seven years have passed since that day, and still I love to talk. I love to talk to listeners who call, or to those whom I meet when I visit their cities. I love to talk to youngsters and senior citizens. I love to talk with people of different backgrounds, different cultures, different beliefs. And I love to encourage them to talk, because as much as I love to talk, I also love to listen to others. I love to hear listeners' stories like the ones in this book and discover their hearts through their words.

It always seems easier to keep silence. What will happen if you tell someone the truth about how you feel? What if what you're feeling is something that might make the other person angry? What will be the cost? Will there be a reward? The answers come to me from my listeners . . .

Stuart and his wife had been married for seventeen years. One evening just before bed, Stuart's wife handed him a slip of paper.

"It was a list, Delilah," Stuart wrote. "Things she thought I wasn't doing enough, and other things I did too much. She had made a list. I blew up. I told her she was overreacting to little things, and walked out of the room."

Stuart stalked through their house, seething. The silence roared in his ears. But as time passed, he cooled down, and he realized there was nowhere else he wanted to go. He soon found himself standing in the bedroom doorway.

"I said, 'Can we talk?' My wife looked up at me and nodded. I told her, 'These things on the list may be true, but they still seem like small matters to me. I want to know more . . . They're important to you, so I want to understand.' We ended up sitting on the bed talking until morning. It wasn't easy. Sometimes it was painful, but we were communicating at a depth we had never reached before.

"As the sun was rising and the bedroom windows turned bright, my wife turned to me and said, 'You know, if you hadn't come back in the room tonight, I would have left you.'

"That night of talking had saved our marriage. Those few hours were the most precious of our seventeen years. I used to take time for granted. I won't do it again."

Stuart's wife showed a lot of courage, sharing what was weighing on her heart. Gather enough little things, and they can be too heavy to bear. Stuart was courageous, too, to risk the pain, to be open to listen, to take responsibility and change. These people took the risk, realized there is a time to speak, and were blessed.

So often it takes a crisis in order to find out what we have to say. Listen to what happened to Amaris and her mother.

One day in February I came home and found my mother lying on the concrete basement floor, unconscious and bleeding.

Terrified, I dialed 911 and begged them to hurry. I knew she was going to die right there in front of me. I hurriedly called my sisters and my father, knowing none of them could make it to the house in time. It was her and me.

I had never been close to my mother. I never felt she loved me, even when she said it. We didn't exactly get along; it was as much my fault as hers, maybe more. But as I stood over her, waiting, helpless, for the ambulance to arrive, I suddenly cried out, "Mama, you can't die! I need you! I love you!" Just as I said it, I realized that I meant it. It was almost as shocking as the accident.

My mother was carried to the nearest emergency room to be treated for severe head trauma. The doctors told us later they hadn't expected her to live. She spent twenty-nine days in rehabilitation. The doctors were amazed at her recovery.

I was relieved she was getting better, but I couldn't free myself from the image of her lying there on the basement floor. I was terrified to go to sleep; when I closed my eyes, I saw her again. I felt tremendously guilty about not coming home a few minutes earlier, and ashamed of wasting almost twenty-five years not telling her how much she means to me.

Everyone kept reminding me I had saved her life and I should not beat myself up. But I knew things weren't going to get better for me until I talked to my mother.

She couldn't speak clearly for some time after the accident, but finally she came home. I sat before her and poured out my heart. I told her how scared I was and how sorry I am for not being a better daughter. I told her I love her, and I meant it. She encouraged me to try to forget that picture in my head. She thanked me for saving her. Most of all, she told me she loves me, and I believe her.

On past Mother's Days I gave her meaningless gifts, if any. This Mother's Day, I've decided to give her something she hasn't had and only I can give her—my love.

Amaris is lucky. She was awakened to her love for her mother, and she was blessed to have her mother there to accept that love and return it.

At times we get a last chance to speak up. Jeff got such an opportunity when his father was diagnosed with advanced colon cancer.

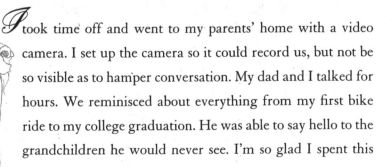

took time off and went to my parents' home with a video camera. I set up the camera so it could record us, but not be so visible as to hamper conversation. My dad and I talked for hours. We reminisced about everything from my first bike ride to my college graduation. He was able to say hello to the grandchildren he would never see. I'm so glad I spent this time with my dad, and taped it. My father said good-bye in a way that was comfortable for him, and now my children will get a glimpse of this wonderful man who gave me so much. I got to say everything I wanted to tell my dad. I'll never have to say, I wish I had told him . . . because I did.

Speaking up, or just taking an opportunity to talk, can change your life, enrich a relationship, or save both. But sometimes, as Donna discovered, speaking up can just be about giving someone a hand, and this can be rewarding too, in more ways than one.

One night I stopped at a drive-through on my way home from work to pick up something for dinner. While I was waiting for my order, I noticed that the truck in front of me had a large tree limb caught under it. I got to worrying that the friction from the limb on the pavement might cause a spark and ignite the gas tank or something. Though I felt a little funny doing it, I decided I wouldn't be able to rest unless I did something. So, I got out of my car and walked up to the side of the truck, making eye contact with the driver in his rearview mirror.

I told him what I had seen and asked if I could pull the limb free of his truck. He grinned and said, "Sure." I jerked the limb from under the truck and dragged it to a nearby hedge, then hurried back to my car, sure that he thought I was some kind of nutcase.

When he drove away, I pulled up to the window and opened my billfold. But the young lady in the window said, "There's no charge. The gentleman in the truck paid for your order. He said it was for a 'random act of kindness.'"

We don't always get a direct reward for speaking up, as Donna did. But go ahead and do it anyway!

My kids get embarrassed because I know the names of people all around us, including the people who work in the drive-through window at our local McDonald's, and I know their stories, too. Terrie is a grandma five times over. She knows I like my broiled chicken burger without mayo and with extra barbecue sauce.

Cindy works at the bank. Her mother recently passed away. Her young children go to school with mine. Robert works at the corner hardware store. He saves the broken and split bags of fertilizer for me and sells them to me at a great price. He saves plants that are past their prime and gives them to me, knowing I'll try to nurse them back to health in my garden. He has two children whom he misses every day; they live with their mother in Oregon. His ex-wife married his ex–best friend. He battles diabetes and has a heart as big as the world.

I have traveled all over the country and talked with incredible people. I've chatted with recording artists and interviewed superstars like Elton John and Bette Midler. I've gossiped with Donny Osmond and even met my childhood heartthrob David Cassidy. And maybe most important of all, I've shared rich conversations with wonderful people all around me. All because I love to talk.

I wonder if Mrs. Brown knows how miserably her duct tape failed.

A Time to Gather Stones Together

A couple of thousand years ago, "a time to gather stones together" made perfect sense. When that biblical verse was written, the Israelites spent a great deal of time gathering stones. They gathered them for two main reasons. The stones were used as construction materials, and, by gathering them, they cleared land for planting vineyards and olive orchards and grain.

The thick wall they built around Jerusalem served quite a few purposes. Obviously it was a protective barrier, a means of keeping their many enemies out. It was also a boundary that defined who they were, a container that held them together as both a nation and a religious people.

Within the wall they built their homes, so the wall wasn't just a barrier but a neighborhood—a place where neighbors lived and raised their families side by side. Each family who lived in the wall was responsible for the upkeep of that portion of the structure. They also took turns patrolling for signs of possible danger—sort of an ancient block watch. Imagine what our cities would be like today if we had preserved at least the wall dwellers' attitude and shared in the responsibility of watching out for our neighbors. Crack dealers wouldn't stand a chance of roping young kids into doing their dirty work under the watchful eyes of dedicated townsfolk.

The city's design was brilliant, with many gates leading into and out of the community. Each gate had a purpose. For example, if you wanted to take your sheep to market from the pastures outside of the city, you passed through the "sheep gate." You didn't have to worry about dirtying some lady's fine shoes with doo-doo, because this gate was to be used only for the passage of sheep. There was a gate that led to the bathing ponds, and another through which fishermen brought their day's catch. The Golden Gate opened into the holy Temple, the sacred place of worship of the Most High God. Built beneath the walls of the city were secret water tunnels that ensured a fresh supply should the city ever come under siege.

When I ponder the fact that these folks didn't have machinery—no backhoes for digging foundations, no cranes to lift great stones, no saws to cut them to fit together snugly, no flatbed trucks to transport them—I am amazed. We have dozens of power tools in our basement, but I can't figure out how to build a simple box for my paints. The people then must have had an incredible commitment to one another, to their community, and to their faith in order to create such beauty and order out of piles of rocks. To gather stones together was to undertake a grueling task for the purpose of building a stronger, more secure, more unified community.

Look around today and you can still find people who are willing to be stone gatherers. In Habitat for Humanity, for one, people sacrifice their time and their resources to build homes for low-income families. Red Cross volunteers dig out and rebuild communities destroyed by fire, earthquake, hurricane, and flood. Thousands of generous volunteers spend countless hours feeding, changing, and holding orphans in third world countries.

In your own town, stone gatherers give up their evenings at home to attend school board meetings, city council meetings, planning committees. You'll find them in nursing homes, talking and listening to seniors others have forgotten. You will find them at Head Start programs, helping underprivileged children learn their ABCs.

Stone gatherers quietly pick up trash someone else tossed in the park. You'll see them holding the hands of little girls in Brownie uniforms, tying knots on tent poles with Boy Scouts, teaching water aerobics at the YMCA. Today, stone gatherers are people who help others and build our community.

The stone gatherers of ancient Jerusalem might have had another motive for gathering, besides building their community or preparing their land for planting. Like every modern child who's ever walked along a beach or climbed a rocky path through the forest, perhaps some of those people gathered stones because they were reminders of their land or their travels, or maybe just because they were beautiful. Stone gatherers don't always have a noble reason. Sometimes they're just people who like to collect rocks.

My father had what is today called an addictive personality. I know all about that—I inherited mine from him. When he became engrossed in a project, his new passion took over and consumed him; it's all he wanted to do. Problem was, it often took over our house as well.

At one point he built a small boat—a pram, it was called. He made the forms, soaked the wood to bend it for the hull, hammered and nailed and sealed and painted a nice, neat, tidy wooden boat. Everyone who saw it told him what a great boat it was. A few folks offered to buy it. So, my dad became a boat-builder.

He built more forms and soaked more wood, and within weeks our yard was filled with half-finished prams. You couldn't get out to play on the swing set without winding and dodging among boat skeletons and boat planks. He gave a few of his high-quality crafts to our relatives, and he sold a few to friends, and then he lost interest. As quickly as he had become a boatbuilder, he stopped. Half-finished boats littered our yard for years.

When I was three or four Dad became fascinated with rocks. He and a few of his friends became rock hounds. He would hike into the hills and mountains of Oregon, or pack us all up and take us to the beach to look for agates or quartz or chunks of petrified wood.

With a small electric motor and a coffee can, he made a rock tumbler. He would load rocks in this contraption, along with a coarse powder, and switch it on. The machine tumbled the rocks like clothes in a dryer, and the powder polished them to a glassy finish. When he took them out and buffed them with a soft cloth they were absolutely spectacular. They shone with brilliant reds and veins of yellow and bright green. The translucent agates seemed to glow.

We marveled at Dad's rocks. He decided that if these few

were so wonderful, more would be more wonderful. But one little tumbler could do only so much. So he built another, and then another. Soon he had everyone he knew looking for unusual and beautiful rocks to polish. Now he decided he needed special saws so he could slice rocks that were large enough and expose the beauty held captive inside.

Dad was completely obsessed with his stones. He created special forms and poured some kind of resin into them, then he set the finished, shining stones into the resin to hold them in place. Out of these forms he created paperweights and desk sets with little penholders. He glued stones into metal clasps for necklaces and earrings. He set them into the bowls of big brandy snifters and gave them as gifts to folks who liked their drinks "on the rocks."

Dad pretty much took over the house with his rock collection. We had boxes of polished rocks, tables covered with molds and gift pieces, cans of pumice. He set the tumblers up under the stairs, and there they ran all night, turning and thumping and polishing the treasures inside. My bedroom was just above the staircase. Every night I fell asleep to the cadence of motors whirring and rocks banging.

Somewhere among my things I have a thin slab of moss agate that Dad cut and polished. It's milky white with a delicate landscape formed by moss trapped inside. If you hold it up to the light it looks like a black-and-white photograph of an ancient redwood forest. It is so beautiful, I'm tempted to start collecting rocks. I wonder if Dad left the plans for his rock tumblers around anywhere.

Some stone gatherers (the non-rock-collecting kind) are unsung for the things they do to make life better. My listeners have written to me about them. Whether they're celebrities or the kid down the street, their work blesses us all. Judith, who is a stone gatherer herself, wrote about a man who returned and carried on the good he was receiving.

In the summer of 1997 I spent two weeks in Hungary, in a little town north of Budapest called Feisgood. I went there with Habitat for Humanity International to build seven duplex houses, which would house fourteen families. One of the men we were helping build his new home arrived one morning with a huge black kettle, a tripod to hang it from, and several bags of food. He gathered scrap wood and built a fire and filled the kettle with water from the well. Using a stack of lumber as his table, he cut up meat and vegetables from his bags and threw it all into the kettle. He spent all morning cooking his homemade—or should I say "site-made"—Hungarian stew. When it was time for our lunch break we gathered around the kettle. He stood so proud next to that kettle, and as he filled each of our bowls he thanked us through our interpreter. The stew was fantastic! It not only filled our stomachs but it filled our hearts as well. We couldn't have received a more appropriate thank-you or a richer reward.

Sometimes it seems that everyone today is obsessed with celebrity. Entire magazines and TV shows are devoted to people who've achieved fame and fortune. The power this gives to these men and women is enormous. And it also gives them an opportunity to be extraordinarily effective stone gatherers, if they choose to. But so often, unable to see beyond their own interests, they don't take the opportunity their good fortune has given them. That's why I like this story from Kathy, about how a person we all know took the time and trouble to enrich one life.

$\mathcal{I}$'m a registered nurse, working on an infectious disease floor, and over the last nine years I've been honored to share the final moments of life with many wonderful people. One particular young man, who was dying of AIDS, spent many, many weeks with us and became a dear friend to me. I spent

many nights at his bedside holding his hand and discussing life, love, our place in the grand scheme of things, and yes, even death and dying.

One night when I came to work, he was extremely excited. "Kathy, you'll never guess who called me this morning. Elton John called me!"

I thought, Yeah, right, sure he did, but I didn't say that. Instead I joshed him: "What did they put in your chemo today?" He laughed but assured me that it really did happen and Elton said he would call back in a few days.

A few days later he again told me that Elton John had invited him to attend a huge AIDS benefit concert at Madison Square Garden. He was so happy. I still wasn't convinced, but as the days went on it became the talk of the floor.

As time passed the young man became thinner and thinner and more and more ill. But it became his goal in life to make it to this concert. He managed to get strong enough to go home just in time for the trip, which, it turned out, was for real.

Elton John had arranged everything—my friend was flown to New York and put up in a luxurious hotel. He got to meet Elton and hang out with him and his friends. He was driven to the concert in a huge white limo, and of course, he had a backstage pass.

He returned from New York happy, but within weeks he

was back with us; his condition had deteriorated. Still he talked and talked about his wonderful trip.

Sadly, this young man's life slipped away in the early morning hours just before Thanksgiving. He died surrounded by family and friends and his favorite night nurse, me. His favorite Elton John CD played in the background.

Apparently this whole wonderful expedition began when the young man's cousin visited Atlanta. While she was there, she gave Elton John's doorman a note telling Elton what a huge fan her cousin was and that he was suffering from AIDS. Elton got the note and made that telephone call that changed this young man's life. I will always be grateful to this busy, world-famous star, who took the time and trouble to ease the final days of my patient, my friend.

Stone gatherers, and stones, don't have to be big to count. Lori wrote about one of the biggest little events of its kind.

I'm a member of a sorority that raises money for cancer research. A few weeks ago we had our annual yard sale. A little boy about seven came up and was looking at a typewriter we had priced at $5. He took off on his bike and returned in a short while with $5 in change, bought the typewriter, and

looked around for something else to buy. He found something else for fifty cents. Well, we were going to just let him have both for the $5, but he said, "No, I want to pay the full price." He put his hand in his pocket and pulled out twenty-one cents. "I'd also like to donate this—my mom has cancer." Well, everyone was speechless. Finally, I managed to say, "Thank you." We didn't get a chance to get his name. I wish I could have done something more for this little boy with such a big heart.

Stone gathering helps to bring people together, whether it's a group of volunteers making dinner at a soup kitchen or a famous singer giving a young man his dream. But for Dee and Keith, stone gathering (the actual, picking-up-stones kind) brought them to the realization that they had already been brought together. The stones told the story.

My husband and I had gone up into the mountains to get away from the daily grind. I'm an avid rock collector. I fill my pockets with them every time we go someplace that has (to my eye) pretty rocks. We were walking along a river that had spilled over its banks not long before. The ground was strewn with boulders and rocks of all shapes, sizes, and col-

ors. Keith had walked ahead, about a hundred yards from me, I noticed as I stooped to pick up an interesting and pretty rock. It was white quartz with a blood red vein running through it. I placed it in my pocket and looked up to see where Keith had gone.

I saw him bend down and pick something up. I hurried up to meet him and we walked on together, enjoying the river and trees and the beautiful day God had given us. As we got back to the van he said, "I found something for you. I thought you might like this rock." I looked, and noticed that Keith's rock was similar to the one I had found. I took mine out of my pocket. It was the only rock I had picked up that day. I held them side by side, and found the place where the red vein in his rock ran and matched mine to it. They interlocked exactly! They were part of the same rock.

That was ten years ago. To us, this experience was a signal from God about our love. When God wants two people to join, even if they're a million miles apart, He will lead them to each other.

I'm so grateful . . . God has allowed me to be a part of so many lives, by radio. And through this connection I've also learned what joy there is for the gatherer of stones . . . there is no greater satisfaction than knowing you have helped a little, or built something that will benefit someone besides yourself. Sometimes I feel that I'm living thousands of lives at once, that I'm in a massive extended family that gathers at the end of each day to share its celebrations and trials. We share our joys and sorrows, our peaceful transitions and our chaotic emergencies. . . . My show is no longer a meeting of entertainers and listeners. We are all listeners.

I remember vividly one cold night in March—I was on the air. An e-mail popped up on my screen that I knew I had to respond to at once. It was from a listener named Steve. His son, also named Steven, had gone out to party with friends. It was the night before his twenty-second birthday. He had decided to leave his car at home and let his friends drive, since he planned to start his birthday celebration early, with more than one drink. After an evening of bowling and drinking, Steven's friends brought him safely home, and even made sure he reached his own room. But Steven's long night was only beginning. His father gave me the details of what happened.

When his friends left him, Steven found that he wasn't ready to go to sleep. He wanted a cigarette, but he had none left. He was feeling fine, and thought his head was clear enough that a drive to the mini mart, a couple of miles away, wouldn't be a great risk.

Steven left the silent house, got into his car, and drove the frosty road to the store. It was just after midnight. So far, so good. He bought his cigarettes and started back. But now his luck ran out. About a half mile from home, he lost control of his car, which ran off the road and hit a utility pole. Steven wasn't wearing his seat belt, and he was hurled through the open driver's window and into the icy waters of Stumpy Lake.

Now, what Steve's dad called "amazing things" began to happen. It seems there were stone gatherers in the neighborhood that night. A married couple named Nix, who set out every morning in the wee hours to deliver newspapers, had left home a little late for their rounds. They were driving separate cars because they served separate neighborhoods, but they drove together to the paper pickup point, along the same deserted road that Steven had driven along just a few minutes earlier. Something flashed as their headlight beams swept the woods at the side of the road, and both Nixes hit their brakes immediately. They saw a car, broken and mangled, resting in the brush. Without a second thought for their own safety at such an hour, they pulled over and stopped. You see, this was the same spot on that dark road where their son's car had skidded and crashed through the Virginia woods barely a year before.

The demolished car was empty, but they knew the driver had to be nearby; no one could have walked away from such a wreck. Mrs. Nix got on her cell phone and called the police. Mr. Nix found a flashlight in his car. Because of their own ordeal, he knew these woods intimately, and he had a hunch. He fought his way through the undergrowth toward the lakeshore. As he approached, Mr. Nix heard a sound from the lake and headed for it. He waded into the icy water, and there he found Steven, submerged, with only his legs visible. He plunged his hands into the lake, caught hold of Steven's sweatshirt, and pulled his head above water. Carefully, tenderly, he held Steven's head for over a half hour, until help arrived. At the hospital Steven was placed on life support. He had suffered multiple head and facial fractures. His right eye socket was crushed. He was unconscious and near death. The doctors said his chances of survival were slim. Still, he hung on to life, and after a while, his vital signs improved to the point that the emergency team removed the respirator. But he lay in a coma.

Now the waiting began. Steven's dad decided to send out a call for support and help. That's when he sent his e-mail message to me, asking me to pass his request for prayers on to the listeners, as he'd heard me do before, and giving me his phone number. When I saw the message, I picked up the phone immediately and called him. We put our conversation on the air and, Steve says, "I was flooded with e-mail from all over the country—total strangers offering their prayers for Steven." For the rest of the night, I prayed, along with millions of others, for Steven's survival.

Days passed and Steven remained unconscious. The doctors prepared his family for the worst; even if he survived, he might not completely return to them.

His dad wrote to me later: "On the tenth day of his coma, I was approaching his room in the ICU. The nurse saw me coming and called out, 'Hurry up!' She got up on Steven's bed and yelled in his face, 'Wake up, Dad's here.' He opened his one good eye and looked up at me and said, 'I love you, Dad.' The nurse threw me a box of tissues."

Steven was coming back to life. He understood and communicated with his therapists, moved his hand, and raised his leg on command. His neurosurgeon called it a miracle. When Steven slipped beneath the freezing waters of the lake, hypothermia set in. His radically lowered body temperature plus his many skull fractures, which relieved the pressure of his swelling brain, saved his life. And of course, there was the arrival of two people, stone gatherers, who could not pass by the scene of certain tragedy, no matter what their own lives demanded of them.

And then there were the rest of us, all over the country, who were given the opportunity to become stone gatherers in attendance that night. Who knows how much our prayers played a part in Steven's survival? At the very least, Steven's dad gave us a chance to be our best.

Today, Steven is back at school and work, and except for some loss of vision in one eye, he has completely recovered. And his dad says he doesn't believe Steven has taken a drink of alcohol since that night. He feels blessed. And so do all of us.

A Time to Love

When I was a child, my mother taught me how to sew. To the casual observer, this is not a profound statement. But to anyone who knows how to sew, or to anyone who has ever tried to teach such a tedious skill to a child, or to anyone who knew that I was much more inclined to climb trees and play football with my older brother, the fact that my mother taught me how to sew is amazing.

If you've ever tried to handle that flimsy paper they use for sewing patterns you know it's about as easy to work with as flypaper. The first thing you must do is take the delicate pattern out of its small envelope and unfold it (it will never, ever go back into the same package, so don't even bother trying). You then arrange the odd-shaped pieces of paper on your fabric, and with straight pins secure the paper to the cloth. Sounds simple enough, but you have to bear in mind that each piece of fabric is different, and the pattern pieces must be arranged so the finished garment won't look like a crazy quilt. The annoying paper would stick to my fingers or rip and I would get *so* frustrated, and beg Mom to let me give up. She would tell me to set it aside for a while, and when I wasn't so frustrated, she would have me back at the cutting board.

When I would whine, "Why can't we buy clothes like everyone else?" she would lovingly explain that when you sew you can be much more creative, and you can have a more complete wardrobe. She didn't harp on the fact that we were poor and my father didn't give her enough money to purchase fashionable clothes for us; she made homemade clothes sound like a luxury.

Then came the cutting. Mom was left-handed. I was right-handed. Just showing me how to cut the fabric and patterns together was difficult for her, but she patiently demonstrated, then switched the scissors and handed them to me. My hand hurt from the heavy metal shears, and my back hurt from bending over the table. At first my edges were ragged and uneven, but with practice I learned to deftly cut the cloth into perfect pieces.

Then came the sewing machine. Mom's machine was at least twenty years old; it didn't have the fancy gadgets or attachments like the ones she lovingly admired at the local Sears store. It was made of heavy metal and had about a thousand moving parts. She told me that you had to learn to love and care for your machine. I heard an awful lot of swearing when she sewed. I figured it was part of her special relationship with the technology. It took me weeks to figure out how to thread the foolish thing, and a few more to figure out how to get the bobbin thread wound and held in place under the machine. I don't know how many times I sat in front of it, thread wound around my hands and the chair I was sitting in, the spool rolling across the floor. Mom would pat my back, take the thread, begin to wind it back on the wooden spool, and say, "Keep trying."

Finally, she showed me how to sew the pieces together. She made me sew each seam with big, loopy stitches; she called it basting. I called it a waste of time. She wanted to make sure I got it right, and as I later discovered, it was much easier to rip out the big loopy stitches than the tiny final seams. Once two pieces were joined together to her satisfaction, she showed me how to sew the final seams. What would have taken her minutes took me several hours. Instead of taking the material from me and finishing it herself, she said, "Sis, this is going to be so beautiful when you're done!" When a seam came out crooked, or when one arm of a shirt ended up two inches longer than the other, she would send me for the seam ripper, to tear it out and do it again. I would whine and complain and try to convince her that no one would notice if one sleeve was a bit longer than the other. She'd have no part of it.

I would work a little longer, a little harder, and after a while I would have a new blouse, a new skirt, a new pair of jeans. She taught me how to use buttons and beads and rhinestones to decorate my designs. I started my first year of high school with an incredible wardrobe, all thanks to the skills Mom taught me. She didn't let me give up.

I watched my mom as she sewed, bent over her machine with a cup of stale black coffee and a cigarette within reach. Late into the night you could hear the hum of her machine as she pushed yards of satin or suede or cotton or linen or Naugahyde through that contraption. She upholstered chairs and couches and settees for people in our town. She made prom dresses and wedding dresses and baby dresses for her children and half the population of Reedsport as well.

I never learned to sew like my mother. I cannot upholster a love seat or fashion a boat sail, as she did. But I did learn to sew. I have created hundreds of curtains and drapes and pillows for the many homes I've lived in. I made my wedding dress to wear when Doug and I were married. I sewed the layette for my babies' bassinets. One day I hope to make wedding dresses for both my daughters.

One of my favorite parts of the Bible, Paul's first letter to the Corinthians, contains, maybe, the world's best definition of love: "Love is patient, love is kind, it is not jealous, it does not boast and it is not arrogant. It does not act unbecomingly, it does not seek its own, it is not provoked, it does not take into account a wrong suffered, it does not rejoice in evil but rejoices with the truth. Love bears all things, believes all things, hopes all things, endures all things. Love never fails." Love is pretty amazing.

Most people who call my show to dedicate songs of love are experiencing a feeling. They think that because they have a heart filled with an overpowering emotion, they're experiencing love. Perhaps they are, but I've learned that love is far more than an emotional experience, far more than a powerful feeling. Feelings and emotions come and go—they change like the weather. Love stays long after the feelings and the emotions fade.

When I was a rebellious teen, there were probably times my mother didn't feel an ounce of love for the destructive young woman who was running headlong into heartache, but she didn't give up on me. There are times when the children we're adopting pour out the pain and anger and rebellion in their hearts, and I don't feel the love and joy I thought I would when we started down this path; but I won't give up on them.

There have been times in our marriage when the romance and passion that overwhelmed us when we first said, "I do," were as far away as east is from west, but we didn't call it quits. We got help, and we talked and we cried and we worked hard to hold it together, even when the feelings of love were lost in frustration and anger and disappointment.

Love is patient. It doesn't give up. Love is kind. It doesn't give up. Love bears all things. It doesn't give up. Love never fails.

Love taught me how to sew . . .

Love is the all-purpose element. It works anytime, anywhere, from birth to death, from romance to real life, for every generation. With the help of my listeners and my friends, I offer here some times of love . . . some as big as the universe, some as small as can be. But when love is involved, there are no insignificant acts . . . every time you love someone even a little bit, something gigantic happens.

Because adoption is so much a part of my life, I have a special place in my heart for those who take on the responsibility of raising a child who needs a safe and nurturing home. I love this story of how Lorraine and her husband went to meet the mother of the child they were about to adopt, and the wonderful ways they chose to prepare for that meeting.

$\mathscr{W}$e had waited for a year and a half to adopt our second daughter. We had been chosen by a birth mother, but there were complications with the adoption, so I had accepted in my heart that we wouldn't get the baby until she was about a year old.

Then, when we knew she was due to be born in just a few weeks, we got a call from our caseworker, saying that the birth mother wanted to meet us immediately. We were quite nervous, and not too eager, but we decided that if that's what she wanted, we could do it. So, with my husband's dad driving us, we traveled all night to the city where she lived. We wondered what she would be like, and worried that she might not like us, or that we might say the wrong thing. We wondered if we would meet all her expectations for the parents of her unborn child. Her caseworker was to be there in the room with us, and be the mediator, if need be. If we all of a sudden didn't know what to say or do, he would keep the meeting flowing.

As we waited in the small office, sitting on the edge of the sofa, we were getting more nervous by the minute. What would we say to the woman who had chosen to give her newborn child to us? Such a precious treasure from heaven, and such a selfless young woman. Finally the caseworker said, "She's coming now." She walked in, wearing a brownish floral one-piece jumper. We immediately exchanged smiles and warm, embracing hugs. With nothing said, it was an instant bonding of spirits, brought together by the one growing in her womb. There were no awkward pauses or uncomfortable moments as we all began to ask one another questions.

I asked her, "Did you have any names picked out?" She said the name, and I told her we would include it somewhere in the child's name. She smiled. In that brief time, we had become friends.

When it was time to go, we presented her with a special music book because she was a singer, and a very special necklace—it was really two necklaces made as one. We gave her half of it, and the other half we kept, for the special little girl who was to be born in just a few weeks.

The caseworker asked her if there was anything else she would like to ask us. She said she couldn't think of anything. He turned to us and my husband spoke up. "Could you sing us a song, so we could share with our baby how beautiful your voice is?" She smiled and said, "I'd love to." She moved forward to the edge of her chair, and looked into our eyes, and sang "Baby Mine." The room was filled with tears of love and joy.

I always knew I wanted to be an adoptive mom, but as anyone who has adopted a child knows, I had my fears and doubts.

Would I be able to love an adopted child to the same depth and with the same quality of commitment as I loved my biological children? Could I bond with this person from another family—even from another culture? How would I know when I had truly become a mother to this child, rather than just a caretaker like all the others? I prayed about it, and watched for signs, and waited . . .

Soon after we adopted our new son, Manny, it was time for our annual vacation to Lake Shasta. I had high hopes of spending time with him, looking for ways to make him a part of our family. At the same time, I was tired and ready for some downtime for myself. I intended to just relax, unwind, and enjoy the beauty of nature. I took my sketch pad, pencils, and a pencil sharpener so I could work on some sketches I had in my mind. I wanted to lie in the sun (using sunblock, of course), sip iced tea, and draw.

But quiet time was not to be. On our first night in the houseboat on the lake, Manny slipped while climbing a ladder, caught his finger in the railing on the way down, and sliced the end of it off. He was so brave, and kept saying, "I'm OK, Mom, don't worry," but I turned instantly into a blubbering, inconsolable wreck.

Houseboats don't move fast enough for emergency dashes across a giant mountain lake, but an angel in a ski boat appeared as if from nowhere and, responding to our frantic waving and shouting, pulled alongside. He never hesitated, but got us aboard his boat and took us on a wild ride back to the marina. Doug and I thanked him profusely and ran off to our car with Manny.

I clutched Manny's hurriedly bandaged finger tightly as Doug drove us down the mountain and into Redding to find the hospital. Finally, in the emergency room, a nurse cleaned Manny's poor finger and administered a shot of Novocain to it, in preparation for suturing. Then she left us, saying she'd be right back; another, more seriously injured person had just been brought in. And so we waited. And waited . . . for what seemed hours. Until, I was sure, the Novocain must be wearing off.

Finally, a different nurse from the first arrived with a suture kit. She got right to work, swabbing Manny's finger again with antiseptic. Manny said, "Uh, I think I might need another shot," but she paid no attention and set to sewing.

Watching Manny's face contort with pain was agonizing for me. I began to cry. "Oh, Mom, it hurts so much," he said.

I whirled on the surprised nurse in a fury. "WHAT PART OF 'I NEED ANOTHER SHOT' DO YOU NOT UNDERSTAND?" She stared up at my face—I am taller than many people—and beat a hasty retreat for the medicine locker.

In that moment I knew I would never be a caretaker or baby-sitter or a foster anything to Manny. This was my son, and he was hurting, and I was truly, completely—and for-ever—his mother.

When a friend gets sick, the first thing we all want to know is, what can I do? We rush around, buying books, sending flowers, cooking food. Sometimes, though, the most important and powerful thing we can do is just be there, loving them. My friend the recording artist Kenny Loggins had an opportunity to give one suffering person what only he could give, his presence. Just by showing up, he gave a young woman a reason to get well.

It was the summer of 1977. I received a phone call at home shortly after dinner one night from a doctor. He introduced himself as Dr. Sullivan and told me he'd been working for a few months with a young girl named Laurie. Laurie was suffering from anorexia. She was declining rapidly and Dr. Sullivan was frantic to find anything that might help. He noticed a photo of me on her hospital room wall and she told him she was a fan of my music. Though he realized it was a long shot, he called me to ask if I would consider visiting her at the hospital.

Honestly, I was a bit dumbfounded and even a little frightened by the responsibility. What words of wisdom might I have hiding inside that could possibly make any difference? But something told me to at least try, so I agreed to go by the hospital that same night.

It was about nine when I got there, and a night nurse quickly ushered me into the girl's room. I sat quietly beside her bed, studying her as she slept. Laurie was only seventeen, and even though she had lost much of her dark brown hair from her illness, I could still tell she'd once been a pretty girl. But what really caught me off guard was her tiny body; she was down to a shocking fifty pounds. She had deep circles under her eyes and an eerily skeletal face with almost transparent skin.

Sitting there in the dimly lit room, nervously waiting for her to awaken, I racked my brain for something I might say, something important, possibly even inspirational, but unfortunately I was coming up with nothing. I felt more self-conscious with each passing moment.

Then she awoke, and for our first few minutes together we simply smiled at each other. I could tell she was exhausted by her ordeal and embarrassed by her situation, yet excited by my presence. Her doctor had prepared her for my visit, but even as she tried to make eye contact with me, she was so weak she could barely lift her head. For a while there I honestly wasn't sure my visit would amount to much, but gradually we began to talk to each other like two old friends picking up where we had left off. The color seemed to reenter her face and she became more animated as she talked about her friends and family, her fatigue, and her condition. I felt the energy of the room begin to change from despair to hope, and a kind of fog seemed to lift from her eyes.

When I left, I asked her to come visit me when she got out of the hospital. This was extremely out of character for me; I'm normally a very private person. But I was so moved by this girl and her struggle that I wanted to do whatever I could to help. She promised she'd call me when she got back on her feet.

Two weeks later Dr. Sullivan called with good news: "I don't know what you said to her, but Laurie's a new girl. She has transformed before our eyes. She's started eating and is already gaining weight. Thank you."

I know now that something more than words passed between us that night, some sense of spirit. We connected, simply by sharing who we really were.

About six months went by before I heard from Laurie. Then, one afternoon quite unexpectedly, she called me from her new job at a gift shop and invited me to meet her for lunch. As I entered the restaurant, I was pleasantly surprised to see a very different Laurie. She had gained weight. She looked happy, healthy, and excited as she told me her plan to become a teacher. "I want to make a difference in the world," she told me, and I couldn't help but believe she would.

Laurie was my first experience of the amazing healing power in our hearts and what we have to give when we simply reach out to one another with love.

Kenny

How do you know when you've found your true love, your soul mate, the person you want to be with for life? "Oh, you'll know" doesn't really work as advice, does it? My listener Teresa's advice might be, Know what you're looking for. Or, You'll know it when you see it.

*D*wayne and I had been dating on and off since we were fourteen. This particular night was very special because we had decided to try our relationship again. We dressed up and went to dinner. After dinner, we wanted to do something special and different, so we went to the park. A group of college kids was hanging out together . . . except for one girl. She was overweight and alone. Nearby was a giant magnolia tree with enormous blooms. Dwayne pulled a picnic table over to the tree, climbed up on it, and picked the prettiest flower he could reach. He walked over to the lonely girl and said, "Hello," and handed her the bloom. She was so pleased. He climbed up on the table again and got a flower for me. I knew again all the reasons I wanted to love him.

I try to remind myself every day what is most important to me and the people around me . . . giving love. No matter how busy you are, no "important" work you're obsessed with can do more good in the world. My friend the singer-pianist Jim Brickman wrote me about one of his most significant and satisfying performances.

With nails polished, a fresh hairdo, and a front row seat, my grandma Gert beamed with pride as her grandson James entertained at the piano. This venue was a little different from the concert halls I'm used to—it was the Whitehall North Nursing Home in Deerfield, Illinois, and it was Mother's Day.

I had scheduled a visit to Grandma because, at ninety-five and a half, Grandma wasn't likely to be able to travel to one of my concerts. It pleased me to have a hand in making her Queen for a Day at Whitehall North, as the impresario who brought me to play for her friends.

The piano needed a bit of tuning, but to have time with Grandma I was willing to put up with that. I geared the show to my audience. They hummed right along to the familiar "Twinkle, Twinkle, Little Star" and "Frère Jacques," and I actually saw a few tears of delight. But the real crowd pleaser was "Rainbow Connection," with its beautiful message—you never know what direction life will take you, or what the future has in store, so make every minute count. The warmth of the applause and appreciation I felt coming back to me caught me a little off guard, and I was touched and filled with love. It turned out to be one of my most thrilling onstage experiences.

Grandma passed away two weeks later. I'm so grateful for the gift of sharing those wonderful moments with her, and playing for her and her friends, and I came away even more determined to make every minute count.

Jim

When I first met Doug, I was not the least bit interested in a romantic relationship with him. I had gone through a long, sad string of failed romances and I'd decided to focus my energies on raising my son, building my career, and getting to know God. Doug was a member of the little church I attended in Dedham, Massachusetts, and he was cute enough to attract the attention of several of my younger single girlfriends.

We'd known each other for over a year when he invited my girlfriends and me to attend a gathering at his parents' house one winter afternoon, and the romance began . . .

We were all just sitting around talking, and pretty soon I found myself concentrating on Doug. Strangely, our friends seemed to be fading off into the background. Something he said made me laugh . . . I liked his bright smile. My eyes wandered to his bookshelf and a title, *The Chronicles of Narnia*, jumped out at me. I had never met a guy who had even heard of *Narnia*, much less read it—much, much less bought a copy for himself.

I noticed and appreciated the close relationship he had with his best friend, Billy. I noticed the electricity in the air around us. And while I heard my alarm system—the one I had installed after all those unsuccessful relationships—the music in the air kept me from paying much attention to the little things I wasn't noticing, like the fact that Doug was only twenty-three and an only child.

Just a month after Doug and I started dating I had plans to take Sonny back home to Seattle for Easter and spring break. On an impulse I invited Doug to join us. We flew into Seattle and spent the first few days with my sister. Then we rented a car and drove down to Oregon. I dropped Sonny off at his grandmother's house and Doug and I were alone for the first time since we had met.

We headed west from Portland, out to the coast, my old turf. Doug had never seen the Pacific Ocean, so I took him to one of my favorite beaches, Haystack Rock. We parked the car and made our way down the winding path to the ocean. The sky was typical Oregon gray and a strong wind whipped my hair as we walked. The ocean was majestic and powerful— huge waves crashed on the rocks and sand.

Near the beach we found a small cave, and without a second thought we walked in. We explored the cave for about an hour, climbing around the damp rocks, talking, laughing, and writing our names in the sandy floor.

Outside the cave was a small, sparkling waterfall—a fresh-water stream was cascading over the rocks and down to the ocean. We stood hand in hand as the seagulls soared overhead, and suddenly we noticed we were alone on the beach. We looked down the long stretch of sand—ours were the only footprints in sight.

We climbed atop a rock at the ocean's edge, looking out at the sea, with tall evergreens as sentinels on the hill behind us. Doug wrapped his arms around me and whispered—loud enough for me to hear over the crashing waves—"I love you." I lay my head back on his shoulder, and I knew in my heart that I would be spending forever in his arms. That day, alone with my future husband on the windswept beach, was the most romantic day of my life.

We took photographs while we were there, and when we had them developed I was impressed with how well they turned out. Many months later I painted a large picture of the beach that day, with the cave and the waterfall, and the tall evergreen trees on the hills behind.

Four years later, after we married and had Shaylah, the magic of that romantic day had faded, and we were swept into a storm. No marriage is always sunny, and young Doug, the only child, met older Delilah, the ambitious single mother who loved to control her environment. Doug had never owned a home, had never fixed a washing machine, had never cared for a child, washed the dishes, or shopped for groceries . . . or worried about washing black jeans with a white soccer uniform.

I'd been single with a child for almost eight years and I was used to being in charge. I found it difficult to consider someone else's point of view when making a decision, and it was even harder for me to compromise. I'd always been the one to direct and discipline Sonny, and neither Sonny nor I adjusted well to another parental figure in the picture. I liked my house decorated the way I wanted it: lots of flowers, chintz, antiques, grapevines, and mauve walls. Doug preferred more modern furnishings and lots of blue.

The kids and I had now moved to Rochester to start the syndication of my show. Doug stayed in Boston. Our daily phone calls usually ended in arguments and anger. Our weekend visits were even more volatile. Some of my friends were encouraging me to end our marriage, and Doug's friends were telling him the same thing.

I didn't know what to do. We had seen a marriage counselor but accomplished nothing. Doug seemed happier when the kids and I weren't around. I was certainly happier without feeling constantly resentful.

One day I walked into the radio station completely drained. Doug and I had been up late arguing on the phone the night before and I hadn't gotten enough sleep. "God, just tell me what to do," I begged. Should I hang in there, hoping we could put it back together? Should I throw in the towel and walk away? Since we were already separated because of my job, it would be easy to just keep going in opposite directions. But my heart was breaking. I loved him so much, and though things were bad, I couldn't imagine my life without Doug by my side.

I stopped at my mailbox before walking into the studio and grabbed my memos and a letter from a listener. As I sat down in the studio I picked up the letter to read it. Turning it over, I looked at the return address neatly written in the upper left-hand corner. And then I noticed the stamp. It wasn't a stamp that you stick on a letter. This was the kind of envelope you can buy at the post office, with the stamp already printed on it. At first I couldn't believe my eyes, and then when I stared hard, I dropped the letter and let out a cry. With trembling hands I picked up the envelope and looked again. I hadn't been mistaken. The stamp, printed in the upper right-hand corner, was a photograph of the Haystack Rock beach in Oregon—an exact replica of the photograph we had taken the day we fell in love, with the cave and the waterfall. An exact replica of the picture I had painted to mark that wonderful day. I began to cry so hard my body shook, and I knew God was reminding me of those two sets of footprints, side by side in the sand. I had my answer.

If true love is about sacrifice, then the love of parents for their children must be the greatest love of all. Gina and Michael wrote me about their exceptional sacrifice for their kids, and the exceptional rewards it has brought them.

Three and a half years ago we were blessed with our first son. Twenty-two months later, we were doubly blessed with twin sons. My husband and I are teachers. When the twins were born, we decided that I would stay home with them. Seven months later, we were pregnant with our fourth child, our baby girl. I was home with the three boys every day, and my husband, Michael, felt like he was missing out on major events in their lives. We decided we needed to do something different.

We now share one full-time teaching position. We have one classroom and we split the week, so we both spend two and a half days in the classroom and two and a half days at home. We struggle financially at times, knowing we could be making twice the money, but obviously we feel that raising our children together is much more important than having everything money could buy.

We continually receive compliments on the way we've chosen to raise our children and what loving and caring children they are. In a world where parents are making money a priority, we feel rich with love.

John Lennon said, "Life is what happens while you're busy making other plans." Well, I believe love is what happens while those plans are being completely destroyed. You plan to spend a nice, quiet day relaxing on the beach, and then your best friend calls and asks if you can watch two of her children while she rushes the other to the emergency room because she has an ear infection that won't clear up.

You plan to wear a sexy silk dress out to dinner with your husband, but the baby needs to nurse and then spits up on your shoulder. You plan on a hot night of passion after dinner (wearing the puke-stained dress), but the same baby is now wide awake and wants to play all night . . .

The things I love most about marriage and kids are the things I hate most. Things like getting up at three in the morning to give Shaylah a treatment for her asthma . . . like not getting to bed on time because Sonny wants me to dye his hair blond to match the rest of his soccer teammates.

Things like trying to figure out why Doug hogs all the covers, then kicks them off in the middle of the night . . . things like donning my new black business suit only to have Zacky smear his mashed bananas all over my legs as I dash out to attend a meeting. There are times when I feel tied up and hopelessly entangled in all that wonderful love.

Janis Joplin sang (in "Me and Bobby McGee"), "Freedom's just another word for nothing left to lose." So many people believe that once they're free of the ties that bind them they'll be happier; they will find peace and fulfillment. Maybe they do find something like those conditions, but only for a little while. Michael English has a new song in which he sings something like this: "When I let the cords of love bind me, I am free." This is how I find my freedom, when I am truly free to grow into the woman I'm supposed to be.

Doug and I chose a verse from Ecclesiastes for the theme of our wedding: "A cord of three strands is not easily broken." We even found wedding bands with three golden cords woven together. One of the cords represents Doug, the second is me, and God is the third strand that holds us together.

Though I strain against those cords sometimes—the cords that demand I put my plans on hold in order to attend to the needs of others—I am grateful for them. They keep those I love close to me.

But love isn't just about marriage and family. Love is what happens when you put your time and your energy, your resources and your heart into another person. Maybe it happens with a complete stranger; maybe it happens with someone you've known all your life. I have seen strangers go out of their way to bless my family or me. I have heard amazing stories of sacrifice and love from my listeners and my friends.

It is only in relation to other people that I grow spiritually and emotionally. When I was alone, by myself, doing just what I wanted, I never had to think of others. I could be selfish and self-centered. But I didn't grow when I was alone. I began to grow only when I started giving real love to people.

Getting close to other people has given me the priceless gift of hearing thousands of stories of how love makes a difference, the most important difference, in life. It is the most productive, the happiest, the most healing use of your time.

The verses we used as the themes of this book are true . . . there is a time to every purpose under heaven . . . and I believe that every purpose is served, in every season, by love.

Time runs out. But love never ends. It is the only truly renewable resource—you make more by giving it away.

We don't have all the time in the world . . . not in this world, anyway. Even if you have faith in the next world, as I do, you must feel the same urgency I do. We've all wasted time, withholding love . . . or denying it, or mistaking something else for love. When you finally learn what love is, as I have, you don't want to spend another minute without filling every second with love. Love someone. Start today.

Printed in the United States
By Bookmasters